Hudson Bay Company Marriages
1820-1851

Gail Morin

Copyright 2016

Hudson Bay Company Marriages 1820-1851

** Marriage No. 154-177 for the years 1828-1829 are not found in the Hudson Bay Company Archives register.

**(No 49-50 in 1822)

…, Christy: See Peter Corrigle and Christy

…, Elizabeth: See James Bird

…, Isabella: See Alexander Work and Isabella

…, Margaret and John Parke

…, Mary: See James Inkster and Mary

…, Sally: See James Saunderson and Sally

…, Sarah: See Thomas Thomas and Sarah

Aberlae, Christy: See Joseph Polander and Christy Aberlae

Aberlae, Margarette: See John Meyer and Margarette Aberlae

Aberlae, Marianne: See Nicholas Francois and Marianne Aberlae

Aberlae, Sophie: See Jean Morell and Sophie Aberlae

Aberlae, Susannah: See Bernard Schmidt and Susannah Aberlae

Adams, George and Anne Heywood: No. 245, George Adams and Anne Haywood, were married by Banns at Red River Settlement 25th October 1832, by Rev. D. T. Jones, Chaplain to the Honble. Hudson Bay Company, Witnesses Present: Adam Mowat and Joseph Monkman.

Adams, Mary: See Henry Eustace and Mary Adams

Alder, Mary: See William Saunderson and Mary Alder

Allary, Frances: See William Bruce and Frances Allary

Allary, Mary: See John Swain and Mary Alesie

Allez, Mary: See Grant Forrest and Mary Allez

Anderson, Anne: See James Corrigal and Anne Anderson

Hudson Bay Company Marriages 1820-1851

Anderson, Catherine: See Charles Cook and Catherine Anderson

Anderson, Charles and Ann Berston: No. 166, John Irvine, of the Red River Settlement, and Margaret Park, of the same place, were married in the Rapids Church, by Banns, and with consent of parties, this Twenty third Day of December in the year One Thousand Eight Hundred Forty Seven by me Robert James Missionary. This marriage was solemnized between us John Irvine (his mark X) and Margaret Park (her mark X), In the presence of John Setter and James Park.

Anderson, Christiana: See Robert Houry and Christiana Anderson

Anderson, Elizabeth: See James Sandison and Elizabeth Anderson

Anderson, Elizabeth: See William Sinclair and Elizabeth Anderson

Anderson, Elizabeth: See William Sutherland and Elizabeth Anderson

Anderson, Henry and Sophia Harper: No. 196, Henry Anderson, of the Red River Settlement, and Sophia Harper, of the same place, were married in St.Andrews Church by Banns and with consent of parties this Twenty eight day of March in the year one Thousand Eight hundred and fifty, By me, Robert James Missionary. This marriage was Solemnized between us Henry Anderson (by mark X) and Sophia Harper (by mark X), In the presence of David Sanderson (by mark X) and Henry Erasmus (by mark X).

Anderson, James and Harriot Smith: No. 128, James Anderson, of Red River Settlement, and Harriot Smith, of the same place, were married at the Grand Rapids, by Banns, with consent of Parents and Parties, this Thirty first Day of August in the year one Thousand eight hundred and Forty four, By me, Wm. Cochran Chaplan to the H. H. B. Company. This marriage was Solemnized between us: James Anderson (by mark X) and Harriot Smith, In the Presence of John James Smith and Charles Anderson.

Anderson, James and Jane Truthwaite: No. 234, James Anderson and Jane Truthwaite, both of Red River Settlement, were married by Banns with consent of Parties this 21st Day of February 1832, by William Cockran Assistant Chaplain to the Honble. Hudsons Bay Company, Witnesses Present: Alexander Kennedy Jr. and Jacob Truthwaite.

Anderson, James and Mary a Sauteux Indian Woman: No. 10, James Anderson, of Brandon House and Mary a Sauteux Indian woman of the same place were married at Brandon House this Twenty third Day of January in the Year One thousand eight hundred and Twenty-One, By me John West Chaplain, This Marriage was solemnized between us James Anderson and Mary (x her mark), In the Presence of John Richards McKay and George McRae.

Anderson, John and Mary Dechenay: No. 111, Jane 31, 1826, John Anderson, of Red River, and Mary Dechenay [Desmarais], of the same place, were married by Banns with consent of parties at Red River Colony by David T. Jones, Chaplain to The H. H. B. Company, In presence of Hugh Gibson and James Anderson settlers.

Anderson, Margaret: See Henry Erasmus and Margaret Anderson

Hudson Bay Company Marriages 1820-1851

Anderson, Phoenia: See Richard Favel and Phoenia Anderson

Anderson, Polly: See James Johnston and Polly Anderson

Antill, George and Julia Jefferson: No. 423, George Antill, Bachelor and pensioner, Red River Settlement, and Julia Jefferson, Spinster, of the same place, were married at the Upper Church, by Banns, with consent of Parents and Parties, this 5th Feb 1849, by me, Wm. Cochran, Chaplain to the H. H. B. Co., Solemnized between us George Antill and Julia Jefferson, In the presence of James Rickards and Mary Spense.

Archelle [?], A... and Jeannet Walker: No. 120, A... Archelle, of Strasburg, Germany, and Jeannet Walker, of Scotland, were married by Banns at Red River Settlement, on the 19th day of July 1826, By David T. Jones Chaplain, In the presence of William Cochran and Xavier Esson.

Arcus, Catherine: See William Peebles and Catherine Arcus

Arkus, Nancy: See Donald Spence and Nancy Arkus

Armstrong, Anne: See John Peter Pruden and Anne Armstrong

Asham, Jane: See Adam Mowat and Jane Asham

Ashim, Ann: See Robert Sutherland and Ann Ashim

Ashim, John and Jane Smith: No. 413, John Ashim of Indian Settlement and Jane Smith of the same place were married at the Indian Settlement R.R.S. by banns with the consent of Parents and Parties This seventh Day of March In the year one thousand eight hundred and thirty nine By me Wm. Cochran Asst Chaplain to the H.H.B. Company. This marriage was solemnized between us John (his X mark) Ashim and Jane (her X mark) Smith, In the presence of Joseph Cook and James Smith.

Atkins, John Allen and Margarret Swain: No. 177, John Allen Atkins, of the Red River Settlement and Margaret Swain, of the same place, were married in the Rapids Church by Banns and with consent of Parties this thirteenth Day of February in the year One Thousand eight hundred and forty nine, By me, Robert James Missionary. This marriage was Solemnized between us John Allen Atkins and Margarret Swain (her mark X), In the presence of John Gunn and James Gunn.

Atkinson, George and Ann Stead: No. 132, George Atkinson, of The Red River Settlement, and Anne Stead, of The same place, were married at the Grand Rapids, by Banns, with consent of Parents and Parties this Twenty first Day of November in the year One thousand eight hundred and Forty Four By me Wm. Cochran, Chaplain to the H. H. Bay Company. This marriage was solemnized between us George Atkinson (by mark X), Ann Stead (by mark X), In the presence of Charles Cummings and Cuthbert Cummings.

Atkinson, Henry and Calistique Vidnave: No. 427, Henry Atkinson, R. R. Settlement, and Calistique Vidnave, of the same place, were married at his house, with consent of Parties, this 1st day of March in the year1849, by me, Wm. Cochran, Chaplain to the H. H. B. Co., Solemnized between us Henry Atkinson and Calistique Vidnave, In the presence of Wm. Flett and Sarah Flett.

Hudson Bay Company Marriages 1820-1851

Atkinson, Margaret: See James Robinson and Margaret Atkinson

Atkinson, Sarah: See William Flett and Sarah Atkinson

Atkison, Nancy: See Andrew Robison and Nancy Atkison

Auld, Jane: See John Charles and Jane Auld

Auld, Mary: See William Taite and Mary Auld

Badger, James and Margaret Badger: No. 25, James and Mary Badger, of the Indian Settlement, were married by Banns on the 16th day of March 1836, by William Cockran, 2nd Chaplain Hon. H. B. Co., Witnesses: Joseph Cook and John James Smith.

Badger, Jane: See William Sandison and Jane Badger

Badger, Thomas and Mary Badger: No. 10, Thomas Badger and Mary Thomas, both of the Indian Settlement, were married by Banns on the 10th day of December 1835, by William Cockran, 2nd Chaplain to Hudson's Bay Compy., Witnesses: Joseph Cook and Peter Corrigal.

Baen, Antoine and Justine Marchant: No. 40, Antoine Baen of the Red River Colony and Justine Marchant of the same place were married at Fort Gilbralter By Banns, this First Day of January in the Year One thousand eight hundred and Twenty Two, By me, John West, Chaplain, This Marriage was solemnized between us Antoine Baen and Justine Marchant, In the Presence of Dominique Dominice and Edw. Harrison.

Ballenden, Betsy: See William Rowland and Betsy Ballenden

Ballenden, Harriett: See John Richards McKay and Harriett Ballenden

Ballenden, James and Fanny Lee Lewes: No. 225, James Ballendine and Fanny Lee Lewes, both of Red River Settlement, were married by Banns with consent of Parties on the 8th Day of December 1831, by William Cockran Assistant Chaplain to the ...[missing entry].

Ballenden, John and Sarah McLeod: No. 322, John Ballenden and Sarah McLeod, were married by Banns with consent of parents and parties, at Red River Settlement on the Tenth day of December 1836, by William Cockran, 2nd Chaplain, Hon. Hudsons Bay Company, Witnesses: Alexander Christie, Chief Factor, and E. H. Whiffer Surgeon.

Ballenden, William and Charlotte Bickersleth: No. 130, William Ballenden, of The Red River Settlement, and Charlotte Bickersteth, of the same place, were married at the Grand Rapids, by Banns, with consent of Parents and parties, this Seventh Day of November in the year One thousand eight hundred forty four, By me, Wm. Cochran Chaplain to the H. H. B. Company. This marriage was Solemnized between us: William Ballenden (by mark X), Charlotte Beckersteth (by mark X), In the presence of George Ross and Eliza Isbister.

Hudson Bay Company Marriages 1820-1851

Bannerman, Alexander and No. 189, Alexander Bannerman, of Red River Colony, and Jenott McKay of the same place, were married by Banns with consent of the parents and parties on the 29th day of December 1829, by David T. Jones, Chaplain and Missionary, In presence of Donald Murray and Robert McBeath.

Bannerman, Ann: See Ann Bennerman

Bannerman, Donald and Janet Matheson: No. 249, Donald Bannerman and Janet Matheson, were married by Banns at Red River Settlement, 29th November 1832, by Rev. D. T. Jones Chaplain to the Honble. Hudsons Bay Company, Witnesses Present: Angus Matheson and Donald Murray.

Banon, Philijune: See Charles Bushe and Philijune Banon

Barban, Peter and Margarret Daniel: No. 176, Peter Barban, of the Red River Settlement and Margarret Daniel, of the same place, were married in the Rapids Church by Banns and with consent of Parties this fourteenth Day of December in the year One Thousand eight hundred and forty Eight, By me, Robert James Missionary. This marriage was Solemnized between us Peter Braban (his mark X) and Margarret Daniel (her mark X), In the presence of Cuthbert Cummings and James McKay.
Beads, Elizabeth: See Allan McIver and Elizabeth Beads

Beads, John and Catherine Robelair: No. 137, John Beads, of The Red River Settlement, and Catherine Robelair, of the same place, were married at the Grand Rapids, by Banns, with consent of Parents and parties, this sixth Day of February in the year One thousand eight hundred forty five By me Wm. Cochran Chaplain to the H. H. B. Company. This marriage was Solemnized between us: John Beads (by mark X), Catherine Robelair (by mark X), In the presence of Charles Cummings and John Cummings.

Bear, David and Elizabeth Smith: No. 296, David Bear, An Indian now at Red River, and Elizabeth Smith, also an Indian girl, were married by Banns at Red River Settlement on the 25th day of February in the year 1835, by D. T. Jones Chaplain to The Honble. Hudson's Bay Compy., Witnesses Robert Sandison and Robert Smith.

Bear, Margaret: See George Beard and Margaret Bear

Bear, Mary: See Robert Sanderson and Mary Bear

Bear, Mary: See William Tate and Mary Bear

Bear, Nancy: See Alexander Smith and Nancy Bear

Bear, Nancy: See Robert Stranger and Nancy Bear

Bear, Thomas and Isabella Beardy: No. 5, Thomas Bear and Isabella Beardy, both Indians now at Red River Settlement, were married at Red River on the 3rd day of December 1835, by D. T. Jones Chaplain to The Hon. H. B. Comp., Witnesses: Robert Smith and David Bear.

Hudson Bay Company Marriages 1820-1851

Bear, Thomas and Nelly: No. 256, Thomas Bear, an Indian, and Nelly, his reputed wife, were married by Banns at Red River Settlement the 3rd April 1833, By The Revd. D. T. Jones Chaplain to the Honble. Hudson's Bay Company, Witnesses Present: Robert Sandison and Thomas Bear.

Bear, William and Margaret Tate: No. 4, William Bear and Margaret Tate, both of Red River Settlement, were married by Banns with consent of parties, on the 3rd day of December in the year 1835, by D. T. Jones Chaplain to The Hon. H. B. Co., Witnesses: George Sandison and Robert Sandison.

Beard, George and Margaret Bear: No. 244, George Beard, a Native Indian, and Margaret Bear were married by Banns at Red River Settlement by Banns the 3rd October 1832, by David T. Jones Chaplain to the Honble. Hudsons Bay Company, Witnesses Present: Wm. Robt. Smith and Robert Sandison.

Beardy, Harriette: See Francis Turner and Harriette Beardy

Beardy, Isabella: See Thomas Bear and Isabella Beardy

Beardy, James and Elizabeth: No. 298, James Beardy, A Native Indian now at Red River, and Elizabeth, An Indian Woman, were married at Red River by Banns on the 20th Day of May 1835, by William Cockran Assist. Champlain to The Honble. H. B. Company, Witnesses: John James Smith and Joseph Cook.

Beardy, Mary: See William Cook and Mary Beardy

Beardy, Nancy: See George Prince and Nancy Beardy

Beauchamp, Joseph and Marie Lapoint: No. 375, Joseph Beauchamp, of Red River Settlement, and Marie Lapoint, of the same place, were married by Banns with consent of parties, on the 27th day of December in the year 1837, by David T. Jones, Chaplain to the Honble. Hudson's Bay Company, Witnesses: Geo. Sandison and Frances Cook.

Beck, Mary: See Thomas Lawson and Mary Beck

Begg, Charles and Catherine Spence: No. 127, Charles Begg, of Red River Settlement, and Catherine Spence, of the same place, were married at the Grand Rapids by Banns with Consent of Parents and Parties this Sixteenth day of May in the year One thousand eight hundred and Forty Four, by me Wm. Cochran Chaplain to the Hon. H. B. Company. This marriage was solemnized between us Charles Begg and Catherine Spence, In the presence of Thomas Truthwaite and James Matheson.

Bender, Jacob and Rosette Monnier: No. 33, Jacob Bender of the Red River Colony and Rosette Monnier of the same place were married at Fort Douglas with Consent of Parents, this Seventh Day of November in the Year One thousand eight hundred and Twenty One, By me, John West, Chaplain, This Marriage was solemnized between us Jacob Bender and Rosette Monnier, In the Presence of Walher de Huser, David Monnier, Antoine Brechler, and George McRae.

Hudson Bay Company Marriages 1820-1851

Bennerman, Ann: See James Frazer and Anne Bennerman: No. 55, James Frazer of the Red River Colony and Ann Bennerman of the same place were married by Contract Jany. 18th 1818 and married at the Red River Colony by banns this Nineteenth Day of December in the Year One thousand Eight hundred and twenty two, By me, John West, Chaplain, This Marriage was solemnized between us James Frazer and Ann Bennerman (x her mark), In the Presence of George McRae and Robert Campbell.

Berston, Ann: See Charles Anderson and Ann Berston

Berston, Azgelick: See Peter Keplin and Azgelick Berston

Bethune, Janet: See Donald McDonald and Janet Bethune

Bickersleth, Charlotte: See William Ballenden and Charlotte Bickersleth

Bird, Amelia: See James Taylor and Amelia Bird

Bird, Amelia: See Peter Fiddler and Amelia Bird

Bird, Charlotte: See John Flett and Charlotte Bird

Bird, Chloe: See James Flett and Chloe Bird

Bird, Elizabeth: See James Sinclair and Elizabeth Bird

Bird, Frederick and Ann Garrioch: No. 376, Frederick Bird, Bachelor, of the Red River Settlement, and Ann Garrioch, Spinster, of the same place, were married at the Middle Church by Banns with consent of Parents, on the 21st day of December in the year 1843, by me, Abraham Cowley, Missionary, Solemnized between us Frederick Bird and Ann Garrioch, Witnesses: Gavin Garrioch and Philip Bird.

Bird, George and Anne Thomas: No. 97, George Bird, of Red River Settlement, and Anne Thomas, of the same place, were married on 23 August 1825 by Banns with consent of the parties and parties at R. R. Settlement by David T. Jones Chaplain to the Hudsons Bay Company, In presence of James Bird Esq and Thomas Thomas Esq.

Bird, Henry and Harriet Calder: No. 86, Henry Bird and Harriet Calder were married at Red River Settlemen by Banns on the twenty eighth day of October 1824 by me, David T. Jones, Asst. Chaplain, In the presence of Richard Cook, Charles Mackay.

Bird, James and Elizabeth: No. 19, James Bird, Chief Factor, of Red River Colony and Elizabeth of the same place were married at Red River Colony this Thirtieth Day of March in the Year One thousand eight hundred and Twenty-One, By me John West Chaplain, This Marriage was solemnized between us James Bird and Elizabeth (x her mark), In the Presence of James Monkman and George Harbidge.

Hudson Bay Company Marriages 1820-1851

Bird, James and Isabella Gibson: No. 160, James Bird, of the Red River Settlement, and Isabella Gibson, of the same place were married in the Rapids Church, by Banns, and with consent of parties, This Twenty eight Day of January in the year one Thousand eight hundred and Forty Seven by me Robert James Missionary. This marriage was Solemnized between us: James Bird and Isabella Gibson (her mark X), In the presence of John Bruce and James Cunningham.

Bird, James and Mary Lowman: No. 288, James Bird, late Chief Factor in The Hudson's Bay Compy's Service, and Mary Lowman, now residing at Red River; were married by mutual consent at Red River Settlement on the 22nd day of January in the year 1835, by Wm. Cockran, 2nd Chpln. to The Hon. Hudson's B. Co., Witnesses: Geo. Simpson, Governor, J. D. Cameron, Chief Factor.

Bird, John and Mary MacKay: No. 116, March 29, 1826, John Bird of Red River, and Mary MacKay of the same place were married at Red River Colony by Banns with consent of parties and parents by David T. Jones Chaplain, Present: John Edward Mackay and George Bird.

Bird, Joseph and Betsy Thomas: No. 17, Joseph Bird, of Fort Douglas and Betsy Thomas of the same place were married at Fort Douglas this Thirtieth Day of March in the Year One thousand eight hundred and Twenty-One, By me John West Chaplain, This Marriage was solemnized between us Joseph Bird and Elizabeth Thomas, In the Presence of George Harbidge and James Monkman.

Bird, Letitia: See Charles Mackay and Letitia Bird

Bird, Levi and Jane Thomas: No. 247, Levy Bird and Jane Thomas, were married by Banns at Red River Settlement, 9 Nov 1832 by Rev. D. T. Jones Chaplain to the Honorable Hudsons Bay Company, Present: George Bird and William Thomas.

Bird, Maria: See James Sutherland and Maria Bird

Bird, Philip and Mary Fidler: No. 400, Philip Bird, bachelor, Red River Settlement, and Mary Fidler, spinster, of the same place, were married at the Upper Church, by banns, with consent of Parents, this 4th day of February, in the year of our Lord, 1847, by me, J. Macallum, Solemnized between us Philip Bird and Mary Fidler (her mark X), In the presence of James Cunninham and William Garrioch.

Bird, Thomas and Mary McDermot: No. 30, Thomas Bird and Mary McDermot, of Red River Settlement, were married by Banns with consent of parents and parties on the 21st day of April 1836, by David T. Jones, Chaplain to The Hon. H. B. Compy., Witnesses: Andrew McDermot and John Bird.

Bird, William and Bennie Hay: No. 52, William Bird of the Red River Colony and Bennie Hay of the same place were married at the Church Mission House this Twenty Eighth Day of October by banns in the Year One thousand Eight hundred and twenty two, By me, John West, Chaplain, This Marriage was solemnized between us William Bird and Bennie Hay (x her mark), In the Presence of James Monkman and George Harbidge.

Hudson Bay Company Marriages 1820-1851

Bird, William and Sophia Cochran: No. 159, William Bird, of the Red River Settlement, and Sophia Cochran of the same place were married in the Rapids Church, by Banns, and with consent of parties, This Thirteenth Day of December in the year one Thousand eight hundred and Forty Six by me Robert James Missionary. This marriage was Solemnized between us: (X The mark of) William Bird and (The mark X of) Sophia Cochran, In the presence of John Bruce and Jane Clouston.

Birston, Alexander and Betsey Atkinson: No. 15, Alexander Birston and Betsey Atkinson, were married by Banns at Red River Settlement, on the 31st day of December 1835, by Wm. Cockran, Assist. Chapl. to the Hon. H. B. Compy., Witnesses: Henry Budd and John Lyons.

Birston, Alexander and Janet Tait: No. 237, Alexander Birston and Janet Tait, both of Red River, were married by Banns with consent of Parties this 28th Day of June 1832, by David T. Jones Chaplain to the Honble. Hudsons Bay Company, Witnesses Present: ...

Birston, Alexander and Sally Budd: No.216, Alexander Birston of Red River Settlement and Sally Budd of the same place were married at Red River Church on the 7th day of April 1831, by William Cockran Assistant Chaplain to the Honourable Hudsons Bay Comany, Witnesses Present: Henry Budd and William Birstone.

Birston, Catherine: See William Norne and Catherine Birston

Birston, James and Gizzel Rowland: No. 209, James Birston of Red River Settlement and Gizzel Rowland of the same place were married at Red River Church on the 18th day of December 1830 by David T. Jones Chaplain, Witnesses Present: Peter Garrioch and William Birston.

Birston, Magnus and Nancy Lyons: No. 195, Magnus Birston, Rapids of Red River, and Nancy Lyons, of the same place, were married by Banns with consent of parties at Red River church on the 3rd day of March 1830, by William Cockran, Asst. Chaplain and Missionary, In the presence of Margaret Cummings and Flora McTavish.

Birston, Nancy: See James Vollar and Nancy Birston

Birston, William and Hazelique Marchand: No. 125, William Birston, halfbreed of Red River Settlement, married Hazelique Marchand, a canadian half breed, 8 December 1826 St. Johns, by David T. Jones Chaplain, Present: Andrew Linklater and David Johnston.

Birston, William and Mary Kirkness: No. 265, William Birstone and Mary Kirkness, were married by Banns at Red River Settlement 31st December 1833, by Wm. Cockran, Assistant Chaplain of the Hon. Hudson's Bay Company, Witnesses: John James Smith and Edward Mowat.

Boden, Elizabeth: See George Harbidge and Elizabeth Boden

Boodry, Jean: See Donald McDonald and Jean Boodry

Hudson Bay Company Marriages 1820-1851

Bourke, John Palmer and Nancy Campbell: No. 24, John Palmer Bourke of the Red River Colony and Nancy Campbell of St. Mary's Falls place were married at Red River Colony this Eleventh Day of June in the Year One thousand eight hundred and Twenty-One, By me John West Chaplain, This Marriage was solemnized between us John Palmer Bourke and Nancy Campbell, In the Presence of P. Powell and Robert Thiel.

Brass, Peter and Margaret Daniel: No. 171, Peter Brass, Swan River Hon. Hudsons Bay Co's Service, and Margaret Daniel, of the Red River Settlement, were married at the Rapids Church by __ with consent of Parties, this twenty third day of August in the year One Thousand eight hundred forty Eight, By me, Robert James Missionary. This marriage was Solemnized between us Peter Brass (his mark X) and Margaret Daniel (her mark X), In the presence of Archy Johnstone and William Calder (his mark X).

Brechler, Antoine and Elizabeth Rendesbergher: No. 31, Antoine Brechler of the Red River Colony and Elizabeth Rendesbergher of the same place were married at Fort Douglas, this Fourth Day of November in the Year One thousand eight hundred and Twenty One, By me, John West, Chaplain, This Marriage was solemnized between us Antoine Brechler and Elizabeth Rendesbergher (x her mark), In the Presence of Walher de Huser and Paul Regenberge.

Bremner, Alexander and Elizabeth Twatt: No. 259, Alexander Bremner and Elizabeth Twatt, were married by Banns at Red River Settlement 1st May 1833 by The Rev. D. T. Jones, Chaplain of the Hon. Hudson=s Bay Company, Witnesses Present: John Swain, W. Robt Smith.

Bremner, Joseph and Dorothea Mackay: No. 133, Joseph Bremner, A Native of Carthness, at Scotland, and Dorothea Mackay, of the same place, were married by Banns at Red River Colony on the 9th day of November in the year 1827, by David T. Jones Chaplain the Hon Hudsons Bay Company, Present at the Ceremony: Thomas Thomas, John Gunn
Bremner, Sarah: See Peter Brown and Mary Bremner

Bremner, Thomas and Louisa Sutherland: No. __, Thomas Bremner, bachelor, of Red River Settlement, and Louisa Sutherland, spinster, of the same place, were married in the Upper Church, by special license and with consent of parties, this second day of September, in the year of our Lord, one thousand eight hundred and Forty Seven, By me, Wm. Cochran. This marriage was Solemnized between us Thomas Bremner and Louisa Sutherland, In the presence of John Burke and Demia Caplet.

Brown, Henry and Isabella Slater: Henry Brown, married 6 Feb 1829, Isabella Slater. (HBCA - biography of Henry Brown)

Brown, Isabella: See John Folster and Isabella Brown

Brown, Magnus and Ann Oliver: No. 359, Magnus Brown, of Red River Settlement, and Ann Oliver, of the same place, were married at the Upper Church by Banns with Consent of Parties this Eleventh day of November in the year One thousand eight hundred and Forty One, by me Wm. Cochran Chaplain to the Hon. H. B. Company. This marriage was solemnized between us Magnus Brown and Ann Oliver (by mark X), In the presence of John Macallum and William Brown.

Hudson Bay Company Marriages 1820-1851

Brown, Peter and Mary Bremner: No. 427, Peter Brown, of Red River Settlement, and Sarah Brimner of the same place, were married at the Upper Church, by banns, with consent of parties this Twenty Third day of January In the year One Thousand Eight Hundred and Forty, By me William Cochran Asst. Chaplain to the H.H.B. Company. This marriage was Solemnized between us Peter Brown and Sarah Brimner, In the presence of William Brimner and Levi Bird.

Brown, Thomas and Jane Mowat: No. 401, Thomas Brown, bachelor, Red River Settlement, and Jane Mowat, spinster, of the same place, were married at the Upper Church, by banns, with consent of parties, this 4th day of March, in the year of our Lord, 1847, by me, J. Macallum, Solemnized between us Thomas Brown and Jane Mowat, In the presence of George Sutherland and James Slater.

Bruce, James and Mary McNab: No. 146, James Bruce, A Half Breed of Red River, and Mary McNab, of the same place, were married at Red River Colony by Banns with mutual consent on the 8th day of January 1828, by David T. Jones Chaplain and Missionary, Present at the Ceremony: William Garrioch and Joseph Spence.

Bruce, Matilda: See Donald McKenzie and Matilda Bruce

Bruce, William and Frances Allary: No. 129, William Bruce, A Half Breed Native of Red River Settlement and Frances Andre [Allary], A Half Breed Woman of the same place, were married at Protestant Mission Church of the Red River Colony, by Banns with consent of parties on the 31st day of July 1827, David T. Jones Chaplain to the H. H. B. Company, Present at the Ceremony: William Tait and James Bruce.

Budd, Elisabeth: See William Johnston and Elisabeth Budd

Budd, Henry and Betsey Work: No. 21, Henry Budd and Betsey Work, of Red River Colony, were married by Banns on the 4th day of February 1836, by Wm. Cockran, 2nd Chaplain to The Hon. H. B. C., Witnesses: Anne Cockran and John Mowat.

Budd, Nancy: See Michael Rayn and Nancy Budd

Budd, Sally: See Alexander Birston and Sally Budd

Budidbasker, Anna Berbera: See Rodowick Gtestogg and Anna Berbera Budidbasker

Bunn, Eleanor: See William Thomas and Eleanor Bunn

Bunn, John and Catherine Thomas: No. 179, John Bunn, of Red River Settlement, and Catherine Thomas, of the same place, were married by Banns with consent of parties at Red River Settlement on the 23rd day of July7 1829, by William Cockran, Asst. Chaplain and Missionary, In presence of Thomas Bunn and William Thomas.

Bunn, Sarah: See Ebenezer Sutherland and Sarah Bunn

Hudson Bay Company Marriages 1820-1851

Bunn, Thomas and Phoebe Sinclair: No. 1, Thomas Bunn of the Red River Colony and Pheobe Sinclair, were married at the Rock Depot this Ninth Day of September in the Year One thousand eight hundred and Twenty By me John West Chaplain, This Marriage was solemnized between us Thos Bunn (signed) and Phoebe Sinclair (x her mark), In the Presence of A. Macdonald, Jno. Alley (late of Guernsey), George Harbidge.

Bunn, William and Magdalene Campbell: No. _, William Bunn, Bachelor of Red River Settlement, and Magdalene Campbell, Spinster of the same place, were married in the Upper Church, by Banns with consent of Parents, on the 10th day of October, in the year 1843, by me, Abraham Cowley, Missionary, Solemnized between us John Garrioch and Eliza Campbell, Wtinesses: John McCallum and John Bunn.

Bunsley, Catherine: See George Simon

Burdau, John Baptiste and Mary Lewes: No. 212, John Baptiste Burdau of Red River Settlement and Mary Lewes of the same place were married at the Red River Church on the 8th day of January 1831, by William Cockran Assistant Chaplain to the Honble Hudsons Bay Company, Witnesses Present: Peter Corrigal and George Harcus.

Burke, Margaret: See Charles Stodgell and Margaret Burke

Bushe, Charles and Philijune Banon: No. 31, Antoine Brechler of the Red River Colony and Elizabeth Rendesbergher of the same place were married at Fort Douglas, this Fourth Day of November in the Year One thousand eight hundred and Twenty One, By me, John West, Chaplain, This Marriage was solemnized between us Antoine Brechler and Elizabeth Rendesbergher (x her mark), In the Presence of Walher de Huser and Paul Regenberge.

Buxton, Henry and Frances Thomas: No. 152, Henry Buston, A native of Derbyshire, England, and Frances Thomas, A Half Breed Woman of Red River, were married at Red River Church by Banns with consent of parents and parties on the 12th day of June 1828, by David T. Jones Chaplain and Missionary, Present at the ceremony: James Taylor and William Thomas.

Cadotte, Mushell and Nancy Cochran: No. 113, Mushell Cadotte of Red River Settlement, and Nancy Cochran, of the same place, were married at the Grand Rapids by Banns with Consent of Parents and Parties this Twenty ninth day of November in the year One thousand eight hundred and Forty Three, by me Wm. Cochran Chaplain to the Hon. H. B. Company. This marriage was solemnized between us Mushell Cadotte (by mark X) and Nancy Cokran (by mark X), In the presence of Henry Cochran and Sophia Cochran.

Calder, Betsy: See James Sutherland and Betsy Calder

Calder, Elizabeth: See Kenneth MacDonald and Elizabeth Calder

Calder, Harriet: See Henry Bird and Harriet Calder

Hudson Bay Company Marriages 1820-1851

Calder, Horatio Nelson and Nancy Rein: No. 205, Horatio Nelson Calder of Red River Settlement and Nancy Rein of the same place were married at Red River Church on the 1st day of November 1830, by David T. Jones, Chaplain to the Honble Hudsons Bay Company, Witnesses present: Peter Corrigal and William Tate A.

Calder, James and Maria Gibson: No. 147, James Calder, of The Red River Settlement, and Maria Gibson, of The same place, were married at the Grand Rapids, by Banns, with consent of parties, this Twelfth Day of March in the year One thousand eight hundred and Forty Six, By me, Wm. Cochran Chaplain to the H. H. B. Company. This marriage was solemnized between us: James Calder (by mark X), Maria Gibson (by mark X), In the presence of John Pruden and James Cunningham.

Calder, Margaret: See Thomas Daniel and Margaret Calder

Calder, Margaret: See William Dennet and Margaret Calder

Cameron, Elizabeth: See William Clouston and Elizabeth Cameron

Cameron, Hugh and Mary: No. 221, Hugh Cameron and Mary Indian [?], both of Red River Settlement, were married by Banns, with Consent of Parties on the 26th day of October 1831, by D. T. Jones Chaplain, Witnesses Present: [illegible]

Cameron, John Dougald and Mary: No. 260, John Dougald Cammeron and Mary, an Indian Woman, were married by Banns at Red River Settlement 6th June 1833 by The Rev. D. T. Jones, Chaplain of the Hon. Hudson's Bay Company, Witnesses Present: Augt. Nolin, Andrew McDermot, Fran. M. Dease.

Cameron, Thomas and Sophia MacKie: No. 25, The marriage between Thomas Cameron, a Salteaux, and Sophia MacKie, a Cree, was solemnized at the Church Indian Settlement this 5th day of December 1844. (All signatures not copied)

Campbell, Arthur and Catherine Sutherland: No. 34, Arthur Campbell of the Red River Colony and Catherine Sutherland of the same place were married at Fort Douglas By Banns, this Eighth Day of November in the Year One thousand eight hundred and Twenty One, By me, John West, Chaplain, This Marriage was solemnized between us Arthur Campbell (x his mark) and Catherine Sutherland (x his mark) In the Presence of Donald MacDonald and Samuel Henderson.

Campbell, Duncan and Ann Pruden: No. 152, Duncan Campbell, of the Red River Settlement, and Ann Pruden, of the same place, were married by me at the Rapids Church, by Banns, with Consent of Parties, This Sixteenth Day of November in the year one Thousand Eight hundred and forty Six, by me Rober James Missionary. This marriage was Solemnized between us: Duncan (his mark X) Campbell and Ann (her mark X) Pruden, In presence of Thomas (his mark X) Anderson and Catherine (her mark X) Anderson.

Campbell, Eliza: See John Garrioch and Eliza Campbell

Campbell, Magdalene: See William Bunn and Magdalene Campbell

Campbell, Mary: See James Sinclair and Mary Campbell

Hudson Bay Company Marriages 1820-1851

Campbell, Nancy: See John Palmer Bourke

Campbell, Neil and Ann Munro: No. 394, Neil Campbell, bachelor, Beaver Creek, Swan River District, and Ann Munro, spinster, of the Red River Settlement, were married, at the Upper Church, by special license, with consent of friends, this Fifteenth day of October, on the year 1846, by me J. Macallum. This marriage was solemnized between us Neil Campbell and Ann Munro (her mark X), in the presence of Malcolm Paterson and George Munro.

Chalifoux Therese: See Colin Robertson and Therese Chalifoux

Chalifoux, Angelique: See Hugh Gibson and Angelique Chalifoux

Chalifoux, Isabella: See Francis Heron and Isabella Chalifoux

Chalifoux, Julia: See William McKay and Julia Chalifoux

Charlats, Mary: See Francis Monjeunier and Mary Charlats

Charles, Elizabeth: See John Macallum and Elizabeth Charles

Charles, John and Jane Auld: No. 292, John Charles, Chief Factor in the Hudson's Bay Company's Service and Jane Auld, now at Red River, were married at Red River by mutual consent on the 2nd day February in the year 1835, by David T. Jones, Chapln. to the Honble. Hudson's Bay Compy., Witnesses: George Simpson, Governor and J. D. Cameron Chief Factor.

Charles, John and Margaret McCallum: No. __, John Charles, Esquire, late C. F. of the H. H. B. Company Service, now residing in the Red River Settlement, and Miss Margaret McCallum, a native of Scotland, now in Red River Settlement, were married at the Upper Church, by mutual consent of Parties, on the 1st day of February in the year 1844, By me, William Cochran, Chaplain to the H.H.B.C., Solemnized between us John Charles and Margaret McCallum, Witnesses: Geo. Prince and ....

Chart, Ann: See George Walsh and Ann Chart

Chlory, Mary: See James Spence and Mary Chlory

Chouinard, Elizabeth: See Peter Warren Dease and Elisabeth Chouinard

Christey, Alex and Sophia: No. 366, Alex Christey, an Indian now at Red River Settlement, and Sophia, an Indian woman of the same place, were married by Banns with consent of parties on the 2nd day of August in the year 1837, by David T. Jones, Chaplain Honble Hudson's Bay Company, Witnesses: Henry Budd and Mary Cochran.

Hudson Bay Company Marriages 1820-1851

Christie, Alexander and Anne Thomas: No. 293, Alexander Christie, Chief Factor in the Hudson's Bay Company's Service and Anne Thomas, a native of Moose Factory, James's Bay were married at Red River by mutual consent on the 10th day February in the year 1835, by David T. Jones, Chapln. to the Honble. Hudson's Bay Compy, Witnesses: George Simpson, Governor and J. D. Cameron Chief Factor.

Clouston, Robert and Nancy Sutherland: **Robert Clouston married 2 April 1828 RRS. (Denney)

Clouston, William and Elizabeth Cameron: No. 153, William Clouston, Parish of ... Orkney and Elizabeth Cameron, of Lac la Pluie, were married at Red River Church with consent of parents and parties on the 27th June 1828, by David T. Jones Chaplain and Missionary, Present at the Ceremony: Roderick Mackenzie C.F. and William Garrioch.

Cochran, Elizabeth: See John Irvine and Elizabeth Cochran

Cochran, Nancy: See Mushell Cadotte and Nancy Cochran

Cochran, Sophia: See Humphrey Favel and Sophia Cochran

Cochran, Sophia: See William Bird and Sophia Cochran

Cochran, William and Elizabeth Gibson: No. 383, William Cochran, of Red River Settlement and Elizabeth Gibson of the same place, were married by Banns with mutual consent on the 22nd February 1838, by William Cochran 2nd Chaplain to the Honble Hudson's Bay Company, Witnesses: Robert Inkster and Henry Cochran.

Cocking, Mary: See William Hemmings Cook and Mary Cocking

Cockran, Thomas and Nancy: No. 33, Thomas Cockran and Nancy, of Red River Settlement, were married by mutual consent on the 2nd day of Jun 1836, by David T. Jones, Chaplain to The Hon. H. B. Company, Witnesses: Wm. Tate and William Spense.

Cockran, Thomas and Neetcheethis: No. 188, Thomas Cockran, A Native Indian of Red River Settlement and Neetcheethis, his reputed wife, were married at Red River Church with consent of parties on the 24th day of December 1829, by David T. Jones Chaplain and Missionary, In the presence of William Garrioch and Sarah Thomas.

Cook, Catherine: See James Lyons and Catherine Cook

Cook, Charles and Catherine Anderson: No. 123, Charles Cook, of Red River Settlement, and Catherine Anderson, of the same place, were married at the Grand Rapids by Banns with Consent of Parents and Parties this Thirteenth day of March in the year One thousand eight hundred and Forty Four, by me Wm. Cochran Chaplain to the Hon. H. B. Company. This marriage was solemnized between us Charles Cook and Catherine Anderson, In the presence of Nicholas Spence and William Gaddy.

Hudson Bay Company Marriages 1820-1851

Cook, Charles and Margaret Spence: No. 153, Charles Cook, of The Red River Settlement, and Margaret Spence, of the same place, were married in the Rapids Church, by Banns, with consent of parties, This Twenty sixth day of November in the year One thousand eight hundred and Forty Six, By me, Robert James Missionary. This marriage was Solemnized between us Charles Cook and Margaret Spence, In the presence of Andrew Setter and John (his X mark) Irving.

Cook, Charles and Mary Lyons: No. 27, Charles Cook and Mary Lyons, of Red River Colony, were married by Banns with consent of parties on the 5th day of March 1836, by Wm. Cockran, 2nd Chapl. to The Hon. H. B. Co., Witnesses: Levy Bird and Anne Cockran.

Cook, Charles and Nancy Cook: No. 262, Charles Cook and Nancy Cook, were married by Banns at Red River Settlement 17th September 1833 by Wm. Cockran, Assistant Chaplain of the Hon. H. B. Company, Witnesses Present: Griffith Daniel and Peter Garrioch.

Cook, Elen: See George Houry and Elen Cook

Cook, Elizabeth: See John Kirkness and Elizabeth Cook

Cook, Fanny: See George Flett and Fanny Cook

Cook, Henry and Harriet Garrioch: No. 406, Henry Cook of Red River Settlement and Harriet Garrioch of the same place were married at the Grand Rapids R.R.S. by banns with consent of Parents and Parties This Thirteenth Day of December, In the year one thousand eight hundred and Thirty eight, By me Wm. Cochran Asst. Chaplain to the H.H.B. Company. This marriage was solemnized between us Henry Cook and Harriet Garrioch, In the presence of William Garrioch and Gavin Garrioch.

Cook, Jeremiah and Eleanor Spence: No. 58, Jeremiah Cook of Red River Colony, and Eleanor Spence of the same place were married at the the Church Mission House by banns this Seventh Day of April in the Year One thousand Eight hundred and twenty three, By me, John West, Chaplain, This Marriage was solemnized between us Jeremiah Cook and Eleanor Spence (x her mark), In the Presence of James Spence and Joseph Bird.

Cook, John and Sophia Sandison: No. 318, John Cook and Sophia Sandison, were married at Red River Settlement by Banns on the 15th November 1836, by Wm. Cockran, 2nd Chaplain to the Honble. H. Bay Company, Witnesses: Ann Cockran and John Cockran.

Cook, Joseph and Catherine Sinclair: No. 85, Joseph Cook and Catherine Sinclair were married at Red River Settlement by Banns on the twenty seventh day of October 1824 by me, David T. Jones, Asst. Chaplain, In the presence of William Garrioch, George Harbidge.

Cook, Letitia: See David Flett and Letitia Cook

Cook, Margaret: See Charles Heywood and Margaret Cook

Cook, Margaret: See William Sandison and Margaret Cook

Hudson Bay Company Marriages 1820-1851

Cook, Mary: See William Lisk and Mary Cook

Cook, Nancy: See William Garrioch and Nancy Cook

Cook, Nancy: See William Hodgson and Nancy Cook

Cook, Samuel and Isabella Gaddy: No. 91, Samuel Cook and Isabella Gaddy were married at the Red River Settlement by Banns on the 12th day of April 1825 by me, David T. Jones, Assistant Chaplain, Witnesses: George Harbidge, James Sutherland.

Cook, Samuel and Suzette Short: No. 282, Samuel Cook, of the Red River Settlement, and Suzette Short, of the same place, were married by Banns on the 2nd day of December in the year 1834, by D. T. Jones Chaplain to the Honble. Hudson's Bay Company, Witnesses Present: William Corrigal and Alexander Sletter.

Cook, Sarah: See James Settee and Sarah Cook

Cook, Sophia: See Joseph Halcro and Sophia Cook

Cook, William and Mary Beardy: No. 31, William Cook and Mary beardy, of the Indian Settlement, were married by Banns on the 11th day of May in the year 1836, by William Cockran, 2nd Chapln. H. H. B. Compy., Witnesses: Joseph Cook and John James Smith.

Cook, William Hemmings and Mary Cocking: No. 385, William Hemmings Cook, of Red River Settlement and Mary Cocking of the same place, were married by Banns with consent of parties on the 8th day of March in the year 1838, by William Cochran assistant Chaplain to the Honble Hudson's Bay Company, Witnesses: Thomas Bunn and Wm. Garrioch.
Corrigal, Charlotte: See Hugh Linklater and Charlotte Corrigal

Corrigal, Elizabeth: See David Halcro and Elizabeth Corrigal

Corrigal, James and Anne Anderson: No. 183, James Corrigal, of Red River Settlement, and Anne Anderson of the sam place, were married at Red River Church by Banns with consent of parents and parties on the 24th day of November 1829, by David T. Jones, Chaplain and Missionary, In the presence of James Whitequay and William Garrioch.

Corrigal, James and Catherine Flett: No. 271, James Corrigal and Catherine Flett, were married by Banns at Red River Settlement 11th February 1834, by Wm. Cockran, Assistant Chaplain to the Honble. H. B. Company, Witnesses: Peter Corrigal and John Sletter.

Corrigal, James and Mary Richards: No. 191, James Corrigal, of the Red River Settlement, and Mary Richards, of the same place, were married in St.Andrews Church by banns and with consent of parties this Twentieth day of December in the year one Thousand Eight hundred and forty nine, By me, Robert James Missionary. This marriage was Solemnized between us James Corrigal (by mark X) and Mary Richards (by mark X), In the presence of John Chapman and Archy Johnstone.

Hudson Bay Company Marriages 1820-1851

Corrigal, James and Sarah Stead: No. 175, James Corrigal, of the Red River Settlement, and Sarah Stead, of the same place, were married in the Rapids Church, by Banns and with consent of Parties this Twenty third day of November in the year One Thousand eight hundred and forty eight, By me, Robert James Missionary. This marriage was Solemnized between us James Corrigal and Sarah Stead (her mark X), In the presence of Andrew Mowat and James Foubister.

Corrigal, John and Eliza Firth: No. 169, John Corrigal, of the Red River Settlement, and Eliza Firth, of the same place, were married in the Rapids Church, by Banns, and with consent of the parties, this Sixth Day of April in the Year One Thousand eight Hundred and forty Eight, By me, Robert James Missiionary. This marriage was solemnized between us John Corrigal and Eliza Firth (her mark X), In the presence of Charles Firth and Peter Matheson.

Corrigle, Peter and Christy: No. 62, Peter Corrigle of the Red River Colony and Christy, an Indian Woman of the Same place, were married at the Red River Colony this Fifth Day of June in the Year One thousand eight hundred and twenty three, By me, John West, Chaplain. This Marriage was solemnized, Peter Corrigle and Christy (x her mark), In the Presence of Joseph Bird and William Bird.

Couteau, Josette: See James Swain and Josette Couteau

Cox, John and Anne Taylor: No. 1, John Cox, now at Red River Settlement, and Anne Taylor, a half Breed of the same place, were married by Banns at Red River Colony on the 11th day of November in the year 1835, by William Cockran Assistant Chaplain to The Honble. Hudson's Bay Compy., In presence of: Charles Begg and Angus McLeod.

Cree Indian Woman, Betsy: See James Short and Betsy Cree Indian Woman

Cree Indian Woman, Margaret: See Andrew Spence and Margaret a Cree Indian Woman

Cree Indian Woman, Nelly: See John Scarth and Nelly Cree Indian Woman

Cree Indian Woman, Sally: See Thomas Favel and Sally Cree Indian Woman

Cromertie, John and Catherine Park: No. 415, John Cromertie of Red River Settlement and Catherine Park of the same place were married at the Grand Rapids R.R.S. by banns with the consent of Parents and Parties This Twelfth Day of June In the year one thousand eight hundred and thirty nine By me Wm. Cochran Asst Chaplain to the H.H.B. Company. This marriage was solemnized between us John Cromertie and Catherine (her X mark) Park, In the presence of John Park and John Park.

Cummings, Hannah: See Thomass Sinclair and Hannah Cummings

Cummings, Malcome and Mary Mowat: No. 116, Malcome Cummings of Red River Settlement, and Mary Mowatr, of the same place, were married at the Grand Rapids by Banns with Consent of Parents and Parties this Seventh day of December in the year One thousand eight hundred and Forty Three, by me Wm. Cochran Chaplain to the Hon. H. B. Company. This marriage was solemnized between us Malcome Cummings and Mary Mowat, In the presence of Andrew Mowat and John Sutherland.

Hudson Bay Company Marriages 1820-1851

Cummings, Margaret: See Thomas Logan and Margaret Cummings

Cummings, Margarret: See William Knight and Margarret Cummings

Cummings, Robert and Clemen Harper: No. 393, Robert Cummings, A native of Orkney, North Britain and Clemen Harper, A native of Hudsons Bay, were married by mutual consent, at Beren's River House on the seventeenth day of August, on thousaund eight hundred and thirty eight by me David T. Jones Chaplain to the H. H. B. Company. This marriage was solemnized between us Robert Cummings and Clemen (her X mark) Harper, In the presence of John Lloyd and Mary Ross.

Cummings,Charles and Sarah Garrioch: No. 141, Charles Cummings, of The Red River Settlement, and Sarah Garioch, of the same place, were married at the Grand Rapids, by Banns, with consent of Parents and parties, this Thirteenth Day of March in the year One thousand eight hundred forty five By me Wm. Cochran Chaplain to the H. H. B. Company. This marriage was Solemnized between us: Charles Cummings and Sarah Garrioch, In the presence of John Cummings and John Slatter.

Cunningham, Ann: See Angus Morrison and Ann Cunningham

Cunningham, John and Jane Work: No. 333, John Cunningham and Jane Work were married at Red River Settlement by Banns with mutual consent on the 26th day of January 1837, by David T. Jones, Chaplain to the Honble. Hudson's Bay Company, Witnesses: Archibald Spence and William Work.

Cunningham, Mary: See Thomas White and Mary Cunningham

Curtnis, Mary: See William Flett and Mary Curtnis

Dahal, Alexander and Elizabeth Vincent: No. __, Alexander Dahal, bachelor, of Red River Settlement, and Elizabeth Vincent, spinster, of the same place, were married at the Upper Church, with mutual consent of Parties, on the 18th day of April in the year 1844, By me, Abraham Cowley, Missionary, Solemnized between us Alexander Dahal and Elizabeth Vincent, Witnesses: John Vincent and Thomas Thomas.

Daniel Griffith and Margaret: No. 264, Griffith Daniel and Margaret Daniel, were married by Banns at Red River Settlement 17th December 1833 by Wm. Cockran, Assistant Chaplain of the Hon. H. B. Company, Witnesses Present: George Bremner and Spokun Berens.

Daniel, Edward and Isabella Flavel: No. 150, Edward Daniel of the Red River Settlement and Isabella Flavel of the sam place were married by me at the Rapids Church by Banns with Consent of Parties This Twelvth Day of November in the year one Thousand Eight hundred and forty Six, by me Rober James Missionary. This marriage was Solemnized between us: Edward (his mark X) Daniel and Isabella (her mark X) Flavel, In presence of John Jas. Smith and Mary Smith.

Daniel, Fanny: See Thomas Folster and Fanny Daniel

Hudson Bay Company Marriages 1820-1851

Daniel, Griffith and Madelaine McKay: No. 433, Griffith Daniel, of Red River Settlement, and Madelain McKay of the same place, were married at Grand Rapids, by banns, with consent of parties this Twenty Fifth Day of June In the year One Thousand Eight Hundred and Forty, By me William Cochran Asst. Chaplain to the H.H.B. Company. This marriage was solemnized between us Giffith Daniel and Madelain McKay (her X mark), In the presence of Andrew Thomson and Sarah Morwick.

Daniel, Jacob and Margaret: No. 102, Jacob Daniel, of Red River Settlement, and Margaret Daniel, of the same place, were married at the Grand Rapids by Banns with Consent of Parties this Twenty third day of December in the year One thousand eight hundred and Forty One, by me Wm. Cochran Chaplain to the Hon. H. B. Company. This marriage was solemnized between us Jacob Daniel and Margaret Daniel (by mark X), In the presence of James Morwick and Griffith Daniel.

Daniel, John and Jane Daniel: No. 16, John Daniel and Jane Daniel, of Red River, were married by Banns with consent of parties on the 5th day of Jany. 1836, by William Cockran, 2nd Chaplain, H. B. Compy., Witnesses: Griffith Daniel, Ferdinand McKenzie and Thomas Cockran.

Daniel, Margaret: See Peter Brass and Margaret Daniel

Daniel, Margarret: See Peter Braban and Margarret Daniel

Daniel, Mary: See Andrew Thompson and Mary Daniel

Daniel, Nancy: See Donald Johnstone and Nancy Daniel

Daniel, Thomas and Margaret Calder: No. 379, Thomas Daniel, of Red River Settlement and Margaret Calder of the same place, were married by Banns with mutual consent on the 24th Jan, 1838, by Wm. Cochran 2nd Chaplain to the Honble Hudson's Bay Company, Witnesses: Griffith Daniel and Anne Cochran.

Daniel, William and Betsy Rose: No. 165, William Daniel, of the Red River Settlement, and Betsy Rose, of the same place, were married in the Rapids Church, by Banns, and with consent of parties, this Sixteenth Day of December in the year One Thousand Eight Hundred Forty Seven by me Robert James Missionary. This marriage was solemnized between us William Daniel (his mark X) and Betsy Rose (her mark X), In the presence of Robert Peebles and Cuthbert Cummings.

Daniel, William and Margaret Linklater: No. 115, William Daniel of Red River Settlement, and Margaret Linklater, of the same place, were married at the Grand Rapids by Banns with Consent of Parents and Parties this Sixth day of December in the year One thousand eight hundred and Forty Three, by me Wm. Cochran Chaplain to the Hon. H. B. Company. This marriage was solemnized between us William Daniel (by mark X) and Margaret Linklater (by mark X), In the presence of John Swain and Susate Sletter.

Dansee, Catherine: See Henry Hallett and Catherine Dansee

Hudson Bay Company Marriages 1820-1851

Davidson, John and Margaret Mowat: No. 427, John Davidson, Bachelor, R. R. Settlement, and Margaret Mowat, Spinster, of the same place, were married, by Banns, at the Upper Churchwith consent of parties, this 29th day of March 1849, By me, Wm. Cochran, Chaplain to the H. H. B. Co., Solemnized between us John Davidson and Margaret Mowat, In the presence of Wm. Tait and Margaret Flett.

Davis, Catherine: See John Hodgson and Catherine Davis

Davis, Frances: See John Mowat and Frances Davis

Dazis, Simon and Marie Juliane Peltier: No. 38, Simon Dazis of the Red River Colony and Marie Juliane Peltier of the same place were married at Fort Gilbralter By Banns, this Twenty fifth Day of November in the Year One thousand eight hundred and Twenty One, By me, John West, Chaplain, This Marriage was solemnized between us Simon Dazis and Marie J. Peltier (x her mark), In the Presence of Walther DeHuser and Wm. Todd.

De Boish, Peter and Catherine Spense: No. 28, Peter De Boish and Catherine Spense, of Red River Settlement, were married by consent on the 5th day of March 1836, by Wm. Cockran, 2nd Chapl. H. H. B. Compy., Witnesses: Levy Bird and Anne Cockran.

De Boix, Julie: See George Park and Julie de Boix

De Shawrumn, Otwain and Jane Lambair: No. 445, Otwain De Shawbrumn, of Red River Settlement, and Jane Lambair, of the same place, were married at the Rapids by banns, with consent of Parents and Parties this Eleventh day of January in the year 1841 By me William Cochran Asst. Chaplain to the H.H.B. Company. Solemnized between us Otwain De Sharumn (by X mark) and Jane Lambair, In the presence of Thomas Lambair and William Cochran.

Dease, Mary Anne: See Thomas Logan and Mary Anne Dease

Dease, Peter Warren and Elizabeth Chouinard: No. 434, Peter Warren Dease, Chief Factor, now at Red River Settlement, and Elizabeth Chouinard of the same place, were married at Fort Garry, with consent of parties this This Third Day of August In the year One Thousand Eight Hundred and Forty, By me William Cochran Asst. Chaplain to the H.H.B. Company. This marriage was solemnized between us Peter Warren Dease and Elizabeth Chouinard (by mark X), In the presence of John Charles and Revd. Wm Mason.

Debos, Margaret: See Joseph Favel and Margaret Debos

DeChamp, Baptiste and Margaret Johnson: No. 332, Baptiste De Champ and Margaret Johnson, were married at Red River Settlement by Banns with mutual consent on the 19th day of January 1837, by William Cochran, 2nd Chaplain to the Honble. Hudson's Bay Company, Witnesses: Peter Pruden and Wm. Pruden.

Dechenay, Mary: See John Anderson and Mary Dechenay

Delte, Juliann: See Joseph Freck and Juliann Delte

Hudson Bay Company Marriages 1820-1851

Dennet, Andrew and Mary Martinois: No. 396, Andrew Dennet of Red River Settlement and Mary Martinois of the same place were married at the Grand Rapids R.R.S. by banns with consent of Parents and Parties this Twenty fifth day of September in theyear one thousand eight hundred and Thirty eight, by me Wm. Cochran Asst. to the H. B. Company. This marriage was solemnized between us Andrew (his X mark) Dennet and Mary (her X mark) Martinois, In the presence of Elizabeth Heywood and Ann Cochran.

Dennet, Elisabeth: See William Todd and Elisabeth Dennet

Dennet, Janet: See John Hourie and Janet Dennet

Dennet, Margaret: See John Spence and Margaret Dennet

Dennet, William and Margaret Calder: No. 133, William Dennet, of The Red River Settlement, and Margarret Calder, of The same Place, were married at the Grand Rapids, by Banns, with consent of Parents and parties, this Twenty first Day of November in the year one thousand eight hundred and Forty four By me William Cochran Chaplain to the H. H. B. Company. This marriage was Solemnized between us: Wm. Dennet, Margarret Calder (by mark X), In the presence of John Slatter and Colin Bruce.

Dennet, William and Sophia: No. 200, William Dennet, of Red River Colony, and Sophia, An Indian woman, of the same place, were married at Red River Settlement, by Banns with consent of parties on the 23rd day of March 1830, by David T. Jones Chaplain and Missionary, In the presence of Thomas Halcrow and Elizabeth Slater.

Dennett, Elizabeth: See John Slater and Elizabeth Dennett

Desharim, Francis and Margaret Sandison: No. 421, Francus Desharim, Bachelor, now residing at Manitoba Lake, and Margaret Sandison, of Red River Settlement, were married by Banns, at the Upper Church, with consent of Parents and Parties, this 25th day of January in the year of our Lord 1849, by me, Wm. Cochran, Chaplain to the H. H. B. Co., Solemnized between us Francis Desharim and Margaret Sandison, In the presence of Dominique Pambrun and Wm. Hodgson.

Desmarais, Baptiste and Sophia Erasmus: No. 376, Baptiste Desmarais, of Red River Settlement, and Sophia Erasmus, of the same place, were married at Red River on the 28th day of December in the year 1837, by William Cochran, 2nd Chaplain to the Hon. Hudson's Bay Company, Witnesses present: William Cochran and Thomas Lambert.

Desmarais, Charles and Harriet Favel: No. 253, Charles Desmarais and Harriet Favel were married by Banns at Red River Settlement 7th February 1833, By The Revd. William Cockran, Assist. Chaplain the Honble. Hudson's Bay Company, Witnesses Present: John Spence and Joseph Desmarais.

Desmarais, Francis and Margaret Spence: No. 202, Francis Desmarais, of Red River Settlement, and Harriet Spence of the same place, were married at Red River Settlement by Banns with consent of parents and parties on the 31st day of May 1830, by William Cockran, Asst. Chaplain and Missionary, In the presence of Andrew McChorister and Sarah Budd.

Hudson Bay Company Marriages 1820-1851

Dickson, William and Justine Picquette: No. 23, William Dixson, of Colonel Dixson and Elizabeth his Wife, and Justine Picquette of St. Marys Falls place were married at Red River Colony this Ninth Day of June in the Year One thousand eight hundred and Twenty-One, By me John West Chaplain, This Marriage was solemnized between us William Dickson and Justine Picquette (x her mark), In the Presence of A. Dickson and David Tully.

Donald, Ann: See John McCorrister and Ann Donald

Donald, Charles and Jane Ingham: No. 126, Charles Donald, of Red River Settlement, and Jane Ingham, of the same place, were married at the Grand Rapids by Banns with Consent of Parties this Ninth day of May in the year One thousand eight hundred and Forty Four, by me Wm. Cochran Chaplain to the Hon. H. B. Company. This marriage was solemnized between us Charles Donald and Jane Ingham, In the presence of James Gunn and W. R. Smith.

Donald, Mary: See Andrew McChorister and Mary Donald

Donald, William and Anne Donald: No. 12, William Donald and Anne Donald, both of Red River Settlement, were married by Banns with consent of parties on the 17th day of December 1835, by Wm. Cochran 2nd Chapln to the Hon. H. B. Comp., Witnesses: Anne Cochran and John Cochran.

Donald, William and Mary Harper: No. 193, William Donald, of the Parish of St.Andrews Red River Settlement, and Mary Harper, of the same place, were married in St.Andrews Church by license and with consent of parties this Tenth day of January in the year one Thousand Eight hundred and fifty, By me, Robert James Missionary. This marriage was Solemnized between us William Donald (by mark X) and Mary Harper (by mark X), In the presence of Thomas Scott and John McCorrister (by mark X).

Ducharm, Fanny: See Fanny Ducharm and Thomas Lambier

Duck, Magdalene: See Samuel Henderson and Magdalene Duck

Easter, John and Nancy: No. 217, John Easter an Esquemaux Residing at Red River Settlement and Nancy an Indian woman of the same place were married at Red River Church on the 14th day of June 1831, by William Cockran, Assistant Chaplain to the Honorable Hudsons Bay Company, Witnesses Present: Margaret Cumming and Hannah Cumming.

Erasmus, Henry and Margaret Anderson: No. 197, Henry Erasmus, of the Red River Settlement, and Margaret Anderson, of the same place, were married in St.Andrews Church by Banns and with consent of parties this Sixth day of June in the year one Thousand Eight hundred and fifty, By me, Robert James Missionary. This marriage was Solemnized between us Henry Erasmus (by mark X) and Margaret Anderson (by mark X), In the presence of John Slatter and Peter Rasmus.

Erasmus, Peter and Catherine: No. 110, January 31, 1826, Peter Erasmus, a Native of Norway, and Catherine, a Half Breed, of Red River, were married at Red River Settlement by Banns, with consent of parties, D. T. Jones Chaplain to The Honorable Hudson's Bay Company, In presence of James Whitequay and Peter Corrigal Settlers.

Hudson Bay Company Marriages 1820-1851

Erasmus, Sophia: See Baptiste Desmarais and Sophia Erasmus

Erhler, John and Rosina Plankin: No. 57, John Erhler of Red River Colony, and Rosina Plankin of the same place were married at the the Church Mission House by banns this First Day of April in the Year One thousand Eight hundred and twenty three, By me, John West, Chaplain, This Marriage was solemnized between us John Erhler and Rosina Plankin (x her mark), In the Presence of Griffin Eland and George Harbidge.

Esson, Daniel and Margaret Rose: No. 99, October 25th 1825, David Esson of Stromness, Orkney, North Britain and Margaret Rose, of Naion, Scotland, were married at Red River Settlement by Banns with consent of Parents and Parties, David T. Jones, Chaplain to the Hon. H. B. Company, In presence of Mr. Alexander Ross and George McBeath.

Eustace, Henry and Mary Adams: No. 41, Henry Eustace, Accountant H. B. Company and Mary Adams were married at Pembinah By Banns, this Twenty fourth Day of February in the Year One thousand eight hundred and Twenty Two, By me, John West, Chaplain, This Marriage was solemnized between us Henry Eustace and Mary Adams (x her mark), In the Presence of Wm. W. Hyss, Wm. Forrest, and Paul Regenberge.

Favel, Harriet: See Charles Desmarais and Harriet Favel

Favel, Harriet: See John Saunders and Harriet Favel

Favel, Humphrey and Jane: No. 326, Humphrey Favel and Jane, a native woman, were married the 28 December1836, by William Cochran 2nd Chaplain to the Hon. Hudson's Bay Company, Witnesses: Joseph Cook and Timothy Bear.

Favel, Humphrey and Sophia Cochran: No. 118, Humphrey Favel of Red River Settlement, and Sophia Cochran, of the same place, were married at the Grand Rapids by Banns with Consent of Parents and Parties this Fourteenth day of December in the year One thousand eight hundred and Forty Three, by me Wm. Cochran Chaplain to the Hon. H. B. Company. This marriage was solemnized between us Humphrey Favel (by mark X) and Sophia Cochran (by mark X), In the presence of Samuel Whitford and George Park.

Favel, Jane: See Frances Morasay and Jane Favel

Favel, Jane: See John Spence and Jane Favel

Favel, John and Margaret Swane: No. 404, John Favel, bachelor, Red River Settlement, and Margaret Swane, spinster, of the same place, were married at the Upper Church, by banns, with consent of friends, this 13th day of May, in the year of our Lord, 1847, by me, John Macallum, Solemnized between us John Favel (his mark X) and Margaret Swane (her mark X), In the presence of Thomas Swane and Joseph Hardisty.

Hudson Bay Company Marriages 1820-1851

Favel, Joseph and Margaret Debos: No. 179, Joseph Favel, of the Red River Settlement and Margaret Debos, of the same place, were married in the Rapids Church by Banns and with consent of Parties this First Day of March in the year One Thousand eight hundred and forty nine, By me, Robert James Missionary. This marriage was Solemnized between us Joseph Favel (his mark X) and Margaret Debos (her mark X), In the presence of James Park and John Setter.

Favel, Mary: See James Sandison and Mary Favel

Favel, Nancy: See John James Smith and Nancy Favel

Favel, Peggy: See Peggy Halfbreed Woman

Favel, Richard and Phoenia Anderson: No. 330, Richard Favel and Phoenia Anderson were married at Red River Settlement by Banns with consent of parents on the 17th day of January 1837, by William Cochran 2nd Chaplain to the Hon. Hudson's Bay Company, Witnesses: James Whitford and Anne Cochran.

Favel, Sally: See Magnus Spence and Sally Favel

Favel, Samuel and Elizabeth Irvin: No. 154, Samuel Favel, of The Red River Settlement, and Elizabeth Irvin, of The same place, were married in the Rapids Church, by Banns, with consent of Parties, This Third day of December in the year one thousand eight hundred and Forty Six by me Robert James Missionary. This marriage was Solemnized between us: Samuel (his X mark) Favel and Charlotte (her X mark) Irvine, In the presence of Thomas Lambier and James Park.

Favel, Samuel and Margaret Kipling: No. 404, Samuel Favel of Red River Settlement and Margaret Kipling of the same place were married at the Grand Rapids R.R.S. by banns with consent of Parents and Parties This sixth Day of December, In the year one thousand eight hundred and Thirty eight, By me Wm. Cochran Asst. Chaplain to the H.H.B. Company. This marriage was solemnized between us Samuel (his X mark) Favel and Margaret (her X mark) Kipling, In the presence of Thomas Lambier and James Sandison.

Favel, Thomas and Magdalene: No. 100, Thomas Favel, of Red River Settlement, and Magdalene Favel, of the same place, were married at the Grand Rapids by Banns with Consent of Parties this Twenty Third day of November in the year One thousand eight hundred and Forty One, By me Wm. Cochran Chaplain to the Hon. H. B. Company. This marriage was solemnized between us Thomas Favel (by mark X) and Magdalene Favel (by mark X), In the presence of Malcome Cumming and George Davis.

Favel, Thomas and Sally Cree Indian Woman: No. 15, Thomas Favell, of Beaver Creek and Sally, a Cree Indian Woman of the same place were married at Beaver Creek this Twenty-ninth Day of January in the Year One thousand eight hundred and Twenty-One, By me John West Chaplain, This Marriage was solemnized between us Ths. Favel (x his mark) and Sally (x her mark), In the Presence of Alexr Robertson and Robert Macintosh.

Favel, William and Margaret Moody: No. 192, William Favel, of the Red River Settlement, and Margaret Moody, of the same place, were married in St.Andrews Church by banns and with consent of parties this Third day of January in the year one Thousand Eight hundred and fifty, By me, Robert James Missionary. This marriage was Solemnized between us William Favel (by mark X) and Margaret Moody (by mark X), In the presence of James Park and John Anderson.

Ferguson, Nancy: See Donald McDonald and Nancy Ferguson

Fiddler, Peter and Amelia Bird: Peter Fiddler of Red River Settlement and Amelia Bird of the same Place were married at the middle Church R.R.S. by banns with consent of Parents and Parties This Twentieth Day of December In the year one thousand eight hundred and thirty eight, By me Wm. Cochran Asst. Chaplain to the H.H.B. Company. This marriage was solemnized between us Peter (his X mark) Fiddler and Amelia (her X mark) Bird, In the presence of Henry Hallett and George Bird.

Fidler, Charles and Anne Sunders: No. 101, October 25 1825, Charles Fidler of the Red River Colony, and Marie Saunders of the same place, were married by bans with consent of parties of Red River Settlement by David T. Jones Chaplain to The H.H.B. Company In presence of William Garrioch Schoolmaster and Wm. Norn Settler.

Fidler, Clement and Charlotte Sletter: No. 270, Clement Fidler and Charlotte Sletter, were married by Banns at Red River Settlement 6th February 1834, by Wm. Cockran, Assistant Chaplain, Witnesses: James Tate and William Corrigal.

Fidler, Colette: See George Irving and Colette Fidler

Fidler, James and Elizabeth Linklater: No. 181, James Fidler, of the Red River Settlement and Elizabeth Linklater, of the same place, were married in the Church of the Rapids by Banns and with consent of Parties this fifteenth Day of March in the year One Thousand eight hundred and forty nine, By me, Robert James Missionary. This marriage was Solemnized between us James Fidler (by mark X) and Elizabeth Linklater (by mark X), In the presence of George Taylor and Robert Peebles.

Fidler, John and Susanna Kipling: No. 131, John Fidler, of The Red River Settlement, and Susanna Kipling, of The same place, were married at the Grand Rapids, by Banns, with consent of Parents and parties this Fourteenth Day of November in the year One thousand eight hundred and Forty four By me Wm. Cochran Chaplain to the H. H. B. Company. This marriage was solemnized between us John Fidler (by mark X), Susanna Kipling (by mark X), In the presence of Peter Fidler and Richard Smith.

Fidler, Mary: See John Foulds and Mary Fidler

Fidler, Mary: See Philip Bird and Mary Fidler

Fidler, Peter and Mary Indian Woman: No. 26, Peter Fidler, of Manitobah, and Mary, an Indian Woman of the same place, were married at Norway House this fourteenth day of August 1821, by me John West, Chaplain, signed Peter Fidler and Mary (x her mark), In the presence of Nicholas Garry and Donald Sutherland.

Hudson Bay Company Marriages 1820-1851

Fidler, Thomas and Jane Kipling: No. 223, Thomas Fidler and Jane Kipling both of Red River Settlement, were married by Banns with consent of Parties on the 9th Day of November 1831, by William Cockran, Assistant Chaplain to the Honble Hudson's Bay Company, Witnesses Present: Alexander Kennedy Junr and William Birston.

Firth, Eliza: See John Corrigal and Eliza Firth

Firth, Thomas and Eliza: No. 405, Thomas Firth of Red River Settlement and Eliza Firth of the same place were married at the Grand Rapids R.R.S. by banns with consent of Parties This Thirteenth Day of December, In the year one thousand eight hundred and Thirty eight, By me Wm. Cochran Asst. Chaplain to the H.H.B. Company. This marriage was solemnized between us Thomas Firth and Eliza (her X mark) Firth, In the presence of Edward Mowatt and George Ross.

Flavel, Isabella: See Edward Daniel and Isabella Flavel

Flett, Betsy: See Robert Rowland and Betsy Flett

Flett, Catharine: See John Polson and Catharine Flett

Flett, Catherine: See James Corrigal and Catherine Flett

Flett, David and Letitia Cook: No. 447, David Flett, of Red River Settlement, and Letitia Spence [?], of the same place, were married at the Rapids with consent of Parents and Parties this Twenty Fifth day of January in the year 1841, By me William Cochran Asst. Chaplain to the H.H.B. Company. Solemnized between us David Flett and Letitia Cook (by X mark), In the presence of Gavin Garrioch and William Cook.

Flett, George and Fanny Cook: No. 392, George Flett, of the Red River Settlement and Fanny Cook of the same place, were married by Banns with consent of parents and parties on the seventh day of August in the year one thousand eight hundred and thirty eight, by William Cochran Assistant Chaplain to the Honble Hudson's Bay Company, Witnesses: James Flett and Sally Garrioch.

Flett, George and Mary Ross: No. 440, George Flett, of Red River Settlement, and Mary Ross, of the same place, were married at the Upper Church, by banns, with consent of Parents and Parties this Twenty Sixth day of November in the year 1840 By me William Cochran Asst. Chaplain to the H.H.B. Company. Solemnized between us George Flett and Mary Ross, In the presence of Cuthbert Grant and Francis W. Dease.

Flett, George and Peggy Whitford: No. 69, December 7th, 1823, George Flett, settler, and Peggy Whitford, Whitnesses: George Harbidge, Hugh Polson. Marriages celebrated at the Red River Colony from October 1823 to July 1824 by me, David T. Jones 2nd Chaplain.

Flett, James and Chloe Bird: No. 258, James Flett, a half native, and Chloe Bird, were married by Banns at Red River Settlement the 25th April 1833, By The Revd. D. T. Jones Chaplain to the Honble. Hudson's Bay Company, Witnesses Present: George Flett and Thomas Bird.

Flett, Jane: See James Sutherland and Jane

Flett, John and Charlotte Bird: John Flett of Red River Settlement and Charlotte Bird of the same place were married at the Middle Church RRS by banns with consent of Parents and Parties This fifteenth Day of November In the year one thousand eight hundred and thirty eight, By me Wm. Cochran Asst. Chaplain to the H.H.B. Company. This marriage was solemnized between us John Flett and Charlotte (her X mark) Bird, In the presence of William Flett and James Taylor.

Flett, John and Sophia Spence: No. 28, The marriage between John Flett, a Saulteaux, and Sophia Spence, a cree, was solemnized at the Church Indian Settlement this 265th day of December 1844. (All the signatures not copied)

Flett, Nancy: See William Gibson and Nancy Flett

Flett, Peter and Euphemia Halcrow: No. 284, Peter Flett, of Red River Settlement, and Euphemia Halcrow, of the same place, were married by Banns at Red River on the 27th day of November 1834, By D. T. Jones, Chaplain to the Honble. H. B. Company, Witnesses: Thomas Halcrow and John Gibson.

Flett, Peter and Mary Flett: No. 24, Peter Flett and Mary Flett, both of the Indian Settlement, were married by Banns on the 9th day of March in the year 1836, by William Cockran, 2nd Chapl. H. B. Compy., Witnesses: Joseph Cook and John James Smith.

Flett, Richard and Mary Whitford: No. 291, Richard Flett, An Indian now at Red River, and Mary Whitford, An INdian of the same place, were married by Banns at Red River on the 29th of January in the year 1835, by Wm Cockran 2nd Chapln. to The Hon. Hudson's Bay Compy., Witnesses: Joseph Cook and James Johnson.

Flett, William and Elizabeth: No. 439, William Flett, of Red River Settlement, and Elizabeth Flett, of the same place, were married at the Rapids by banns with consent of Parties this Twenty Fifth day of November in the year 1840 By me William Cochran Asst. Chaplain to the H.H.B. Company. Solemnized between us Wm Flett and Elizabeth Flett (X her mark), In the presence of Donald McDonald and George Ross.

Flett, William and Margaret McNab: No. 239, William Flett and Margaret McNab were married by Banns at Red River Settlement the 31st Day of July 1832, by David T. Jones Chaplain to the Honble. Hudsons Bay Company, Witnesses Present: Archibald Spence and Peter Flett.

Flett, William and Mary Curtnis: No. 424, William Flet, of Red River Settlement, and Mary Curtnis of the same place, were married at the Middle Church, by banns, with consent of parents and parties this Nineteenth Day of December In the year One Thousand Eight Hundred and Thirty nine, By me William Cochran Asst. Chaplain to the H.H.B. Company. This marriage was Solemnized between us William Flett (by mark X) and Mary Curtnis (by mark X), In the presence of Robert Sandison and John Spence.

Flett, William and Sarah Atkinson: No. 416, William Flett of Red River Settlement and Sarah Atkinsonof the same place were married at the Grand Rapids R.R.S. by banns with the consent of Parents This Fifteenth Day of July In the year one thousand eight hundred and thirty nine By me Wm. Cochran Asst Chaplain to the H.H.B. Company. This marriage was solemnized between us Sarah Atkinson and William Flett, In the presence of James Flett and David Flett.

Hudson Bay Company Marriages 1820-1851

Flotooh, Alice Sophie: See Henry Louis Merz and Alice Sophie Flotooh

Folster, James and Jane: No. 132,, James Folster, a Native of Orkney, and Jane, an Indian Woman from the Saskatchewan, were married at Red River Colony by Banns with the consent of the parties on the 25th day of November 1827, by William Cockran Assistant Chaplain to the H. H. B. C, Present at the Ceremony: John Bunn and John Folster.

Folster, Janet: See John Folster and Janet Folster

Folster, John and Flora McDonald: No. 122, John Folster, of Red River Settlement, and Flora McDonald, of the same place, were married at the Grand Rapids by Banns with Consent of Parents and Parties this Twenty Second day of February in the year One thousand eight hundred and Forty Four, by me Wm. Cochran Chaplain to the Hon. H. B. Company. This marriage was solemnized between us John Folster and Flora McDonald (by mark X), In the presence of Thomas Truthwaite and John Gunn.

Folster, John and Isabella Brown: No. 426, John Folster, Widower, R. R. Settlement, and Margaret Burke, Spinster, of the same place, were married at the Upper Church, by license, with consent of Parents and parties, this 8th day of March in the year1849, by me, Wm. Cochran, Chaplain to the H. H. B. Co., Solemnized between us John Folster and Isabella Brown, In the presence of James Brown and Mary Brown.

Folster, John and Janet Folster: No. 72, January 5, 1824, John Folster and Janet Folster, Witnesses: James Livingstone x mark, William Taite x mark. Marriages celebrated at the Red River Colony from October 1823 to July 1824 by me, David T. Jones 2nd Chaplain.

Folster, Thomas and Fanny Daniel: No. 203, Thomas Folster, of the Parish of the Middle District, Red River Settlement, and Fanny Daniel, of the parish of St.Andrews, were married in St.Andrews Church by banns and with consent of parties this Thirtieth day of January in the year one Thousand Eight hundred and fifty one, By me, Robert James Missionary. This marriage was Solemnized between us Thomas Folster (by mark X) and Fanny Daniel (by mark X), In the presence of Angus Henderson and Alexander McBeath.

Folster, William and Maria Pruden: No. 124, William Folster, of Red River Settlement, and Maria Pruden, of the same place, were married at the Grand Rapids by Banns with Consent of Parents and Parties this Twenty Eight day of March in the year One thousand eight hundred and Forty Four, by me Wm. Cochran Chaplain to the Hon. H. B. Company. This marriage was solemnized between us William Folster (by mark X) and Maria Pruden (by mark X), In the presence of Peter Pruden and Peter Fidler.

Forbes, John and Isabel Spence: No. 128, John Forbes of Mea [?] Ireland, and Isabel Spence of Red River Settlement were married by Banns at Red River Settlement on the 3rd day of April 1827, by William Cochran, Assistant Chaplain, In the presence of Joseph Cook and Thomas Halcrow.

Forbister, John and Catherine Robertson: No. 106, December 9th 1825, John Forbister, a native of Stromness, Orkney Islands, Catherine Robertson of Red River Settlement, married at Red River Colony, By Banns with consent of parents and parties by D. T. Jones, Chaplain to The Hon. Hudsons Bay Company, In presence of William Norn and William Garrioch.

Hudson Bay Company Marriages 1820-1851

Forrest, Grant and Mary Allez: No. 79, Mr. Grant Forrest, accountant of New Fort Douglas and Miss Mary Allez, a native of Guernsey, were married at Red River Settlemtn on the seven day of September 1824 by Me, David T. Jones, Asst. Chaplain, In the presence of Robert Parker Pelly, Governor of Assiniboia, Donald McKenzie, Chief Factor, Fort Garry.

Foulds, John and Mary Fidler: No. 100, October 15th 1825, John Folds, of Red River Colony, and Mary Fidler, of the same place were married at Red River Settlement by Banns with consent of theparties, by David T. Jones, Chaplain of the Honorable H. B. Company, In presence of William Garrioch, Schoolmaster and William Norn.

Fouman, Mary Rolfe: See Robert Morris and Mary Rolfe Fouman

Fourniel, Lydia: See John Warring and Lydia Fourniel

Fournier, Justine: See John Wassaloski and Justine Fournier

Fox, Charles and Thurza Stevens: No. 444, Charles Fox, of Red River Settlement, and Thurza Stevens, of the same place, were married at the Rapids, with consent of Parties this Thirty First day of December in the year 1840 By me William Cochran Asst. Chaplain to the H.H.B. Company. Solemnized between us Charles Fox (by X mark) and Thurza Stevens, In the presence of George Stevens and John Mowat.

Francois, Nicholas and Marianne Aberlae: No. 53, Nicholas Francois of the Red River Colony and Marianne Aberlae of the same place were married at the Church Mission House this Seventeenth Day of October in the Year One thousand Eight hundred and twenty two, By me, John West, Chaplain, This Marriage was solemnized between us Nicholas Francois (x his mark) and Marianne Aberlae (x her mark), In the Presence of George Harbidge and Antoine Lutman.

Fraser, Christiana: See Robert Munro and Christiana Fraser

Fraser, James: See James Frazer

Fraser, John and Jane Matheson: No. 419, John Fraser of Red River Settlement, and Jane Matheson of the same place, were married at the Middle Church, by banns, with consent of parties this seventh Day of November In the year One Thousand Eight Hundred and Thirty nine, By me William Cochran Asst. Chaplain to the H.H.B. Company. This marriage was Solemnized between us John Fraser and Jane Matheson, In the presence of Angus Matheson and John Pritchard

Frazer, Barbara: See Donald Matheson and Barbara Frazer

Freck, Joseph and Juliann Delte: No. 73, February 2nd, 1824, Joseph Freck, a Meuron settler and Juliann Delte, Witnesses: George Harbidge, Wildrick Hauffman. Marriages celebrated at the Red River Colony from October 1823 to July 1824 by me, David T. Jones 2nd Chaplain.

Gaddy, Isabella: See Samuel Cook and Isabella Gaddy

Hudson Bay Company Marriages 1820-1851

Gaddy, William and Margaret Garrioch: No. 266, William Gaddy and Margaret Garrioch, were married by Banns at Red River Settlement 14th January 1834, by Wm. Cockran, Assistant Chaplain of the Hon. H. B. Company, Witnesses: Peter Garrioch and John Garrioch.

Garde, Louise: See John Irvine and Louise Garde

Garrioch, Ann: See Frederick Bird and Ann Garrioch

Garrioch, Harriet: See Henry Cook and Harriet Garrioch

Garrioch, John and Eliza Campbell: No. _, John Garrioch of Red River Settlement, and Eliza Campbell of the same place, were married near the Upper Church, by Banns with consent of Parents and Parties, on the 21st day of September, in the year 1843, by me, William Cochran Chaplain in the H. H. B. C., Solemnized between us John Garrioch and Eliza Campbell, Wtinesses: Henry Cook and Gavin Garrioch.

Garrioch, Margaret: See William Gaddy and Margaret Garrioch

Garrioch, Peter and Margaret McKenzie: No. 425, Peter Garrioch, Bachelor, Red River Settlement, and Margaret Burke, Spinster, of the same place, were married at the Upper Church, by license, with consent of parties, this 28th day of Feb in the year1849, by me, Wm. Cochran, Chaplain to the H. H. B. Co., Solemnized between us Peter Garrioch and Margaret McKenzie, In the presence of Anne McDermot, John McLoughlin, and Robert Logan.

Garrioch, Sarah: See Charles Cummings and Sarah Garrioch

Garrioch, William and Nancy Cook: No. 22, William Garrioch, of Swan River, Second Trader, and Nancy Cook of the same place were married at Fort Douglas this Twenty seventh Day of May in the Year One thousand eight hundred and Twenty-One, By me John West Chaplain, This Marriage was solemnized between us William Garrioch and Nancy Cook, In the Presence of George Harbidge and Donald Mathison.

Gibboo, William and Margaret Sinclair: No. 190, William Gibboo, of the Red River Settlement, and Margaret Sinclair, of the same place, were married in the Rapids Church by banns and with consent of parties this Tenth day of December in the year one Thousand Eight hundred and forty nine, By me, Robert James Missionary. This marriage was Solemnized between us William Gibboo (by mark X) and Margaret Sinclair (by mark X), In the presence of Thomas Scott and Charles Firth.

Gibson, Ann: See Donald Sinclair and Ann Gibson

Gibson, Barbara: See James Louis and Barbara Gibson

Gibson, Elizabeth: See William Cochran and Elizabeth Gibson

Gibson, Hugh and Angelique Chalifoux: No. 118, April 28, 1826, Hugh Gibson of Orkney North Britain and Angelique Chalifoux of Red River, were married by Banns with consent of parties at Red River Settlement by David T. Jones Chaplain to Hudson Bay Company, Present: Peter Corrigal and George Harcus, Settlers.

Hudson Bay Company Marriages 1820-1851

Gibson, Isabella: See James Bird and Isabella Gibson

Gibson, Margaret: See John Lyons and Margaret Gibson

Gibson, Maria: See James Calder and Maria Gibson

Gibson, William and Nancy Flett: No. 77, June 29th, 1824, William Gibson and Nancy Flett, Witnesses: Wm. Garrioch and Robert Rowland. Marriages celebrated at the Red River Colony from October 1823 to July 1824 by me, David T. Jones 2nd Chaplain.

Gladu, Margaret: See James McKay and Margaret Gladu

Gladue, Sarah: See William McIntosh and Sarah Gladue

Goboche, Louisa: See David Sandison and Louisa Goboche

Good, Delilah: See John William Sellwood and Delilah Good

Grachu, Lorain: See William Spence and Lorain Grachu

Green, James and Isabella Gunn: No. __, James Green, bachelor of Red River Settlement, and Isabella Gunn, widow of the same place, were married at the Upper Church, by special license, with consent of parties, this Thirteenth day of November, in the year of our Lord One Thousand Eight Hundred and Forty Five, by me, John Macallum, Solemnized between us, James Gunn and Isabella Gunn, In the presence of Thomas McDermot and George Flett.

Grimm, Margaret: See Julien Tunier and Margaret Grimm

Groat, George and Charlotte Spence: No. 301, George Groat, a native of Orkney, now at Red River, and Charlotte Spence, A Half Breed, were married at Red River by Banns on the 30th day of June in the year 1835, by David T. Jones Chaplain to The Hudson's Bay Company, Witnesses: Donald Murray and James Spence.

Gtestogg, Rodowick and Anna Berbera Budidbasker: No. 87, Rodowick Gtestogg, of Wuztumberg in Germany and Anna Berbera Budidbasker, Canton of Berne, Switzerland, were married at Red River Settlement by Banns on the thirteenth day of December 1824, by me, David T. Jones, Asst. Chaplain, In presence of: Peter Riendisbacher, George Harbidge.

Gunn, Catharine: See William McDonald and Catharine Gunn

Gunn, Donald and Margaret Swain: No. 108, January 17, 1826, Donald Gunn, a native of Caithness, Scotland, and Margaret Swain, of Red River, were married by Banns with consent of parties at Forage Plain, Red River Settlement, by D. T. Jones Chaplain to The Hudson's Bay Company, In presence of Joseph Cook and William Sutherland.

Hudson Bay Company Marriages 1820-1851

Gunn, Henrietta: See George Sutherland and Henrietta Gunn

Gunn, Isabella: See Morrison McBeath and Isabella Gunn

Gunn, Margaret: See Angus Matheson and Margaret Gunn

Gunn, William and Isabella Ross: No. 448, William Gunn, of Red River Settlement, and Isabella Ross, of the same place, were married at the Rapids with consent of Parents and Parties this Fourth day of February in the year 1841, By me William Cochran Asst. Chaplain to the H.H.B. Company. Solemnized between us William Gunn and Isabella Ross, In the presence of Donald Gunn and Francis W. Dease.

Guthrie, Thomas and Isabella, an Indian Woman: No. 274, Thomas Guthrie and Isabella, an Indian Woman, were married by Banns on the 1st May 1834, by D. T. Jones Chaplain to the Honble. H. B. Company, Witnesses: James Sandison and Isabella Guthrie.

Halcro, David and Elizabeth Corrigal: No. 199, David Halcro, of the Parish of St.Andrews Red River Settlement, and Mary Harper, of the same place, were married in St.Andrews Church by banns and with consent of parties this Thirty first day of October in the year one Thousand Eight hundred and fifty, By me, Robert James Missionary. This marriage was Solemnized between us David Halcro (by mark X) and Elizabeth Corrigal (by mark X), In the presence of Thomas Sletter and Peter Rasmus.

Halcro, John and Sarah: No. 342, John Halcro and Sarah, his reputed wife were married at Red River Settlement on the 8th day of March 1837, by William Cochran, 2nd Chaplain to the Honble. Hudson's Bay Company, Witnesses: Peter Corrigal and Joseph Cook.

Halcro, Joseph and Sophia Cook: No. 103, Joseph Halcro, of Red River Settlement, and Sophia Cook, of the same place, were married at the Grand Rapids by Banns with Consent of Parents and Parties this Seventh day of July in the year One thousand eight hundred and Forty Two, by me Wm. Cochran Chaplain to the Hon. H. B. Company. This marriage was solemnized between us Joseph Halcro and Sophia Cook (by mark X), In the presence of William Work and John Sutherland.

Halcro, Joshua and Francois Laurain: No. 68, October 31st, 1823, Joshua Halcro, an officer in the company=s service and Francois Laurain a Half caste native woman, Witnesses: C. Cumming, Wm. Garrioch. Marriages celebrated at the Red River Colony from October 1823 to July 1824 by me, David T. Jones 2nd Chaplain.

Halcro, Margaret: See Jerry Mackay and Margaret Halcro

Halcro, Thomas and Charlotte Knight: No. 19, Thomas Halcro and Charlotte Knight, of Red River, were married by Banns on the 21st day of Jany. in the year 1836, by Wm. Cockran, 2nd Chaplain to H. B. Compy., Witnesses: William Corrigal and James Sutherland.

Halcrow, Euphemia: See Peter Flett and Euphemia Halcrow

Hudson Bay Company Marriages 1820-1851

Halcrow, Thomas and Mary Southward Indian Woman: No. 2, Thomas Halcrow of the Red River Colony and Mary a Southward Indian Woman, were married at the Red River Settlement this Twenty-fifth Day of Oct in the Year One thousand eight hundred and Twenty By me John West Chaplain, This Marriage was solemnized between us Thomas Halcrow (signed) and Mary (x her mark), In the Presence of James Bird and George Harbidge.

Halfbreed Woman, Margaret: See Andrew Setter and Margaret a halfbreed Woman

Halfbreed Woman, Peggy: See Michael Lambere and Peggy a halfbreed Woman

Halfbreed Woman, Sennecasso: See Robert Saunderson and Sennecasso Halfbreed Woman

Hallet, Antoine and Jane Spence: No. __, Antoine Hallett, bachelor of Red River Settlement, and Jane Spence, spinster of the same place, were married at the Upper Church, by special license with consent of parties, this Twenty Eighth day of July, in the year of our Lorad, One Thousand Eight Hundred, and Fort Six, by me John Macallum, Solemnized between us: Antoine Hallett and Jane Spence, In the presence of James Spence and David Spence.

Hallet, William and Maria Pruden: No. 355, Henry Hallet, of Red River Settlement, and Maria Pruden, of the same place, were married at the Upper Church by Banns with Consent of Parties this Sixth day of September in the year One thousand eight hundred and Forty One, by me Wm. Cochran Chaplain to the Hon. H. B. Company. This marriage was solemnized between us William Hallet (by mark X) and Maria Pruden (by mark X), In the presence of William Pruden and Cornelius Pruden.

Hallett, Catherine: See David Spence and Catherine Hallet

Hallett, Henry and Catherine Dansee: No. 81, Henry Hallett and Catherine Dansee were married at Red River Settlement on the sixteenth day of October 1824, by me David T. Jones, Asst. Chaplain, In presence of George Harbidge, James Hallett.

Hallett, Henry Junior and Catherine Parenteau: No. 82, Henry Hallett Junior and Catherine Perentau were married at Red River Settlement by Banns on the eighteenth day of October 1824 by me, David T. Jones, Asst. Chaplain, In the presence of George Harbidge, Henry Hallett Senior.

Hallett, Sophia: See James Knight and Sophia Hallett

Hancock, Harry and Mary Ann Ward: No. 156, Harry Hancock, Color Sergeant 6th, of Red River Settlement, and Mary Ann Ward, of the same place, were married in the Rapid Church by License, with consent of parties, This Fifth Day of December in the year one Thousand eight hundred and forty Six by me Robert James Missionary. This marriage was Solemnized between us: H. Hancock and Mary Ann (her X mark) Ward, In the Presence of Samuel Barker and Elizabeth Barker (her mark X).

Hudson Bay Company Marriages 1820-1851

Harbidge, George and Elizabeth Boden: No. 51, George Harbidge of the Red River Colony, School Master to the Church of England, Miss. Society and Elizabeth Boden, of the same place, School Mistress, were married at the Church Mission House by banns with Consent of Parents and the Committee of the above Society, this Eighteenth Day of October in the Year One thousand Eight hundred and twenty two, By me, John West, Chaplain to the H.B.Co. and Superintending Missionary, This Marriage was solemnized between us George Harbidge and Elizabeth Boden, In the Presence of Andrew Bulger and William Garrioch.

Harcus, David and Jane Taylor: No. 151, David Harcus, of the Red River Settlement, and Jane Taylor, of the same place, were married by me at the Rapids Church, by Banns, with Consent of Parties This Twelvth Day of November in the year one Thousand Eight hundred and forty Six, by me Robert James Missionary. This marriage was Solemnized between us: David (his mark X) Harcus and Jane (her mark X) Taylor, In presence of John Jas. Smith and William Stevens.

Harcus, George and Isabella Park: No. 143, George Harcus, of the Island of Pomera, Orkney, and Isabella Park, of Red River Colony, were married at the Lower Church Red River Settlement on the 18th day of December 1827, by D. T. Jones Chaplain and Missionary, Present at the Ceremony: James Whitequay and Andrew Linklater.

Harper, Clemen: See Robert Cummings and Clemen Harper

Harper, James and Charlotte Turner: No. 129, James Harper, of Red River Settlement, and Charlotte Turner, of The same Place, were married at the Grand Rapids, by Banns, with consent of parties, this seventeenth Day of October in the year One Thousand eight hundred and forty four By me Wm. Cochrane Chaplain to the H. H. B. Company. This marriage s solemnized between us: James Harper Charlotte Turner (by mark X_, In the presence: Thomas Truthwaite, Henry Stevens.

Harper, John and Maria Knight: No. 320, John Harper and Maria Knight, were married by Banns at Red River Settlement on the 24th of November 1836, by David T. Jones, Chaplain to The Honble. Hudsons B. Comp., Witnesses: James Knight and John Muir.

Harper, Mary: See William Donald and Mary Harper

Harper, Sophia: See Henry Anderson and Sophia Harper

Harper, William and Anne Taylor: No. 219, William Harper and Anne Taylor, borh of Red River Settlement, were married by Banns with Consent of Parties on the 17th day of August 1831, by David Jones, Chaplain to the Hon'l Hudson's Bay Company, Witnesses Present: James Ballantyne and Wm. Robt Smith.

Hay, Bennie: See William Bird and Bennie Hay

Hay, Thomas and Letitia Spence: No. 449, Thomas Hay, of Red River Settlement, and Letitia, of the same place, were married at the Rapids with consent of Parents and Parties this seventh day of March in the year 1841, By me William Cochran Asst. Chaplain to the H.H.B. Company. Solemnized between us Thomas Hay (by X mark) and Letitia Spence (by X mark), In the presence of Nicholas Spence and Thos. Lambier.

Hudson Bay Company Marriages 1820-1851

Hemmingway, Fredrick and Jane Taylor: No. 173, Fredrick Hemmingway, of the Red River Settlement, and Jane Taylor, of the same place, were married in the Rapid's Church by Banns and with consent of parties, This Twenty fifth Day of September in the year One Thousand Eight hundred and forty Eight, By me, Robert James Missionary. This marriage was Solemnized between us Fredrick Hemmingway (his mark X) and Jane Taylor (her mark X), In the presence of James McCorister and William Stevens.

Henderson, Anne: See Angus Polson and Anne Henderson

Henderson, Jane: See George Sandison and Jane Henderson

Henderson, Janet: See Hugh Polson and Janet Henderson

Henderson, Mary: See Samuel Whitford and Mary Henderson

Henderson, Nancy: See Charles Isham and Nancy Henderson

Henderson, Peter and Charlotte: **Peter Henderson and Charlotte were married 2 Mar 1829, RRS. (List of HBC Marriages, Joanne J. Hughes, c1977) (Denney) (HBCA - biographies)

Henderson, Peter and Eleanor Whitford: No. 120, Peter Henderson, of Red River Settlement, and Eleanor Whitford, of the same place, were married at the Grand Rapids by Banns with Consent of Parents and Parties this Twenty first day of December in the year One thousand eight hundred and Forty Three, by me Wm. Cochran Chaplain to the Hon. H. B. Company. This marriage was solemnized between us Peter Henderson and Eleanor Whitford (by mark X), In the presence of John Hodgson and John Hodgson Jr.

Henderson, Samuel and Magdalene Duck: No. 205, Samuel Henderson, of Fort Alexander River Ounipeg, and Magdalene Duck, of the same place, were married in Fort Alexander with consent of parties this Twenty third day of May in the year one Thousand Eight hundred and fifty one, By me, Robert James Missionary. This marriage was Solemnized between us Samuel Henderson and Magdalene Duck (by mark X), In the presence of James Isbister and Phillip Kennedy.

Henry, Nancy: See James Swain and Nancy Henry

Henry, Nancy: See William Pruden and Nancy Henry

Heron, Francis and Isabella Chalifoux: No. 302, Francis Heron, Chief Trader of the Hudson's Bay Company, and Isabella Chalifoux of Red River Settlement, were married by mutual consent on the 16th day of July in the year 1835, at Red River Settlement, by David T. Jones Chaplain to The Honble. Hudson's Bay Company, Witnesses: Wm. Cockran, Assist. Chaplain, John Macallum, and John Lloyd.

Heywood, Anne: See George Adams and Anne Heywood

Heywood, Charles and Margaret Cook: No. 281, Charles Heywood, a Half Breed of the Red River Settlement, and Margaret Cook, of the same place, were married by Banns at Red River Settlement 18th November in the year 1834, by Wm. Cockran, 2nd Chaplain to the Honble. H. B. Company, Witnesses: Thomas Cockran and Joseph Daniel.

Heywood, Elizabeth: See James Knight and Elizabeth Heywood

Higgs, William Walne and Henrietta Hoerner: No. 54, William Walne Higgs of the Red River Colony and Henrietta Hoerner of the same place were married at the Church Mission House by banns this Seventeenth Day of November in the Year One thousand Eight hundred and twenty two, By me, John West, Chaplain, This Marriage was solemnized between us William Walne Higgs and Henrietta Higgs, In the Presence of Henry Eustace and David Hoerner.

Hodgson, John and Catherine Davis: No. 184, John Hodgson, of the Red River Settlement and Catherine Davis, of the same place, were married in the Rapids Church by Banns and with consent of Parties this Fifth Day of July in the year One Thousand eight hundred and forty nine, By me, Robert James Missionary. This marriage was Solemnized between us John Hodgson and Catherine Davis), In the presence of John Mowat and Peter Henderson.

Hodgson, John and Charlotte Yorkstone: No.139, John Hodgson, A Half Breed Settler, and Charlotte Yorkstone, of the same place were married by Banns, with mutual consent; at the Protestant Church in Red River Settlement on the 4th of December 1827, by David T. Davis Chaplain, Witnesses present: James Inkster and John Inkster.

Hodgson, William and Nancy Cook: No. 182, William Hodgson, of the Red River Settlement and Nancy Cook, of the same place, were married in the Rapids Church by Banns and with consent of Parties this Twenty Second Day of March in the year One Thousand eight hundred and forty nine, By me, Robert James Missionary. This marriage was Solemnized between us William Hodgson and Nancy Cook (by mark X), In the presence of John McDonald and John Hodgson.

Hoemer, Henrietta: See William Walne Higgs and Henrietta Hoerner

Hogue, Aimable and Margarette Taylor: No. 215, Aimable Hogue of Red River Settlement and Margarette Taylor of the same place were marred at Red River Church on the 24th day of March 1831 by David T. Jones Chaplain to the Honourable Hudsons Bay Company, Witnesses Present: Pierre Lablanc and William Bruce.

Holmes, Elizabeth: See James Murray and Elizabth Holmes

Hope, Fanny: See Thomas Thomas and Fanny Hope

Hope, Flora: See William Sanders and Flora Hope

Hudson Bay Company Marriages 1820-1851

Hope, William and Catherine: No. 280, William Hope, an Indian, now at Red River Colony, and Catherine, an Indian woman, were married by Banns with consent of parties on the 22nd of October 1834, by William Cockran 2nd Chaplain to the Honble. Hudson's Bay Company, Witnesses: Joseph Cook and Catherine Cook.

Hourie, John and Janet Dennet: No. 251, John Hourie and Janet Dennet were married by banns at Red River Settlement 2nd January 1833, By David T. Jones, Chaplain to the Honble. Hudson's Bay Company, Witnesses Present: William Dennet and Thomas Halcro Junr.

Houry, George and Elen Cook: No. 143, George Houry, of The Red River Settlement, and Elen Cook, of The same place, were married at the Rapids Church, by Banns, with consent of Parents, this Thirteenth Day of October in the year One thousand eight hundred and Forty Five, By me, Wm. Cochran Chaplain to the H. H. B. Company. This marriage was solemnized between us: George Houry (by X mark), Elen Cook (by mark X), In the presence of George Spence and Charles Cook.

Houry, Robert and Christiana Anderson: No. 371, Robert Houry, of Red River Settlement, and Christiana Anderson, of the same place, were married by Banns with consent of Parties, on the 28th day of November in the year 1837, by William Cochran, 2nd Chaplain to the Hon. Hudson's Bay Company, Witnesses: James Anderson and Mary Halcrow.

Howell, Patience: See William Smith and Patience Howell

Howes, Henry and Jannet Spence: No. 206, Henry Howes [sic], of Red River Settlement, and Jannet Spence of the same place, were married at Red River Church on the 1st day of November 1830, by David T. Jones Chaplain, Witness Present: Peter Corrigal and William Tate, A.

Howrie, John and Margaret: No. 92, John Howrie and Margaret an Indian woman were married by .. at Red River Settlement, 10 May 1825, by David T. Jones, Assistant Chaplain, In the presence of Wm. Garrioch and Wm. Sutherland.

Humbert Droz, Adelgone: See Donald Mackenzie and Adelgone Humbert Droz

Hunter, James and Jean Ross: No. __, James Hunter, Clerk of the Church Missionary Society, and Jean Ross, of Norway House, were married at Norway House, by Special License, with consent of Parents and Guardian, this Tenth day of July in the year of our Lord, one Thousand Eight Hundred and Forty Eight, by me, John Sutherland, Solemnized between us James Hunter and Jean Ross, In the presence of Donald Ross, Wm. Mason, Nicol Finlayson, Frs. Ermatinger.

Hunter, James and Jean Ross: No. 414, James Hunter, Clerk of the Church Missionary Society, and Jean Ross, of Norway House, were married at Norway House, by Special License, with consent of Parents and Guardian, this Tenth day of July in the year of our Lord, one Thousand Eight Hundred and Forty Eight, by me, John Sutherland, Solemnized between us James Hunter and Jean Ross, In the presence of Donald Ross, Wm. Mason, Nicol Finlayson, Frs. Ermatinger.

Indian Woman, Mary: See Peter Fidler and Mary Indian Woman

Hudson Bay Company Marriages 1820-1851

Indian, Bear and Harriet: No. 243, Bear, an Indian and Harriet, his reputed wife, were married at Red River Settlement by Banns the 3rd October 1832, by David T. Jones Chaplain to the Honble. Hudsons Bay Company, Witnesses Present: Wm. Robt. Smith and Robert Sandison.

Indian, Robert and Betsy: No. 213, Robert a Native Indian now Residing at Red River Settlement and Betsey his reputed wife of the same place were marred at the Red River Church on the 10th day of March 1831, by David T. Jones Chaplain to the Honorable Hudsons Bay Company, Witnesses present: Robert Sandison and David Jones.

Ingham, Jane: See Charles Donald and Jane Ingham

Inkster, James and Elizabeth Sutherland: No. 210, James Inkster of Red River Settlement and Elizabeth Sutherland of the same place were married at Red River Church on the 16th day of December 1830 by David T. Jones Chaplain to the Honble Hudsons Bay Company, Witnesses Present: Robert Clouston and John Park.

Inkster, James and Letitia Sutherland: No. 211, James Inkster of Red River Settlement and Letitia Sutherland of the same place were married at Red River Church on the 16th day of December 1830 by David T. Jones Chaplain to the Honble Hudsons Bay Company, Witnesses Present: Thomas Sinclair and William Sutherland.

Inkster, James and Mary: No. 84, James Inkster and Mary, a Cree Indian Woman, were married at Red River Settlement by Banns on the twenty sixth day of October 1824, by me, David T. Jones, Asst. Chaplain, In the presence of John Richard McKay, John MacIntyre.

Inkster, John and Isabella Sandison: No. 252, John Inkster and Isabella Sandison were married by banns at Red River Settlement 31st January 1833, By David T. Jones, Chaplain to the Honble. Hudson's Bay Company, Witnesses Present: William Hallett and Robert Sandison.

Inkster, John and Mary Sinclair: No. 109, January 20, 1826, John Inskster, of Orkney North Britain, and Mary Sinclair, of Red River, were married by Banns with consent of Parties at Red River Settlement by David T. Jones, Chaplain to The Hon. Hudson's Bay Company, In presence of Mr. Thomas Bunn and Mr. Joseph Cook.

Irvin, Elizabeth: See Samuel Favel and Elizabeth Irvin

Irvine, John and Elizabeth Cochran: No. 119, John Irvine of Red River Settlement, and Elizabeth Cochran, of the same place, were married at the Grand Rapids by Banns with Consent of Parents and Parties this Fourteenth day of December in the year One thousand eight hundred and Forty Three, by me Wm. Cochran Chaplain to the Hon. H. B. Company. This marriage was solemnized between us John Irvine (by mark X) and Elizabeth Cochran (by mark X), In the presence of Henry Cochran and Nicholas Spence.

Hudson Bay Company Marriages 1820-1851

Irvine, John and Louise Garde: No. 148, John Irving, of The Red River Settlement, and Louise Garde, of The same place, were married at the Rapid Church, by Banns and with consent of parties, this thirteenth day of September in The year one Thousand eight hundred and forty Six, By me, John Smithurst Missionary. This marriage was Solemnized between us, X the mark of John Irvine and X the mark of Louise Garde, In the presence of D. Gunn and Samuel Tait.

Irvine, John and Margaret Park: No. 166, John Irvine, of the Red River Settlement, and Margaret Park, of the same place, were married in the Rapids Church, by Banns, and with consent of parties, this Twenty third Day of December in the year One Thousand Eight Hundred Forty Seven by me Robert James Missionary. This marriage was solemnized between us John Irvine (his mark X) and Margaret Park (her mark X), In the presence of John Setter and James Park.

Irving, George and Colette Fidler: No. 255, George Irving and Colette Fidler were married by Banns at Red River Settlement the 7th March 1833, By The Revd. D. T. Jones Chaplain to the Honble. Hudson's Bay Company, Witnesses Present: Charles Fidler and David Gerson.

Irving, John and Mary: No. 199, John Irving, of Red River Colony, and Mary, An Indian Woman of the same place, were married by Banns with mutual consent at Red River on the 18th day of May in the year 1830, by William Cockran, Asst. Chaplain and Missionary, In the presence of Peter Corrigal and Nancy Ward.

Irwin, James and Matilda Tate: No. 418, James Irwin, Bachelor, Red River Settlement, and Matilda Tate, Spinster, of the same place, were married at the Upper Church, by Banns, with consent of Parents and Parties, this thirteenth day of November 1848, by me, Wm. Cochran, Chaplain to the H. H. B. Co., Solemnized between us James Irwin and Matilda Tate, In the presence of Phillip Tate and George Tate.

Isbister, Thomas and Mary Kennedy: No. 25, Thomas Isbister, clerk at Cumberland House, and Mary Kennedy of Norway House married at Norway House this Twentieth Day of August 1821, By me Jn. West Chaplain, signed Thos. Isbister and Mary Kennedy, In the Presence of Nicholas Garry and George Simpson.

Isham, Charles and Ann Johnston: No. 319, Charles Isham and Ann Johnston, were married by Banns with consent of the parties on the 23rd day of November 1836, at Red River Settl., by Wm. Cockran, 2nd Chaplain to the H. H. B. Company, Witnesses: Joseph Cook and John Hope.

Isham, Charles and Nancy Henderson: No. 317, Charles Isham and Nancy Henderson, were married at Red River Settlement by Banns with consent of parties on the Tenth day of November in the year 1836, by William Cockran, 2nd Chaplain to the Hudson's Bay Comp., Witnesses: John Hudson and Wm. Gaddy.

Isham, Isabella: See John Spence and Isabella Isham

Isham, James and Anne Isham: No. 31, James Isham and Anne Isham, both of the Indian Settlement, were married by Banns with consent on the 11th day of May 1836, by William Cockran, 2nd Chapln. H. H. B. Compy., Witnesses: Joseph Cook and John James Smith.

Hudson Bay Company Marriages 1820-1851

Isham, James and Mary Isham: No. 17, James Isham and Mary Isham, of Red River Settlement, were married by Banns with consent of parties on the 12th of Jany. 1836, by William Cockran, 2nd Chaplain H. H. B. Company, Witnesses: James Spense and Ann Cockran.

Isham, Price and Hannah Isham: No. 18, Price Isham and Hannah Isham, were married at Red River by Banns on the 12th of Jany. 1836, by William Cockran, 2nd Chaplain H. H. B. Company, Witnesses: James Spense and Ann Cockran.

Isham, Thomas and Nancy: No. 241, Thomas Isham and Nancy, an Indian woman, were married by Banns at Red River Settlement the 22nd Day of August 1832, by David T. Jones Chaplain to the Honble. Hudsons Bay Company, Witnesses Present: Wm. Robt. Smith and Mary Jones.

Ishim, Ann: See John Lambier and Ann Ishim

Jefferson, Julia: See George Antill and Julia Jefferson

Jefferson, Sally: See Joseph Spence and Sally Jefferson

Johnson, David and Betsy Sanderson: No. 67, October 31st, 1823, David Johnson and Betsy Sanderson, Witnesses: Wm. Taite, George Harbidge. Marriages celebrated at the Red River Colony from October 1823 to July 1824 by me, David T. Jones 2nd Chaplain.

Johnson, James and Sally: No. 279, James Johnson, an Indian, now at Red River, and Sally, an Indian woman,, were married by Banns at Red River Settlement, on the 22nd of October 1834, by William Cockran 2nd Chaplain to the Honble. Hudson's Bay Company, Witnesses: Joseph Cook and Catherine Cook.

Johnson, John and an Indian Woman: No. 263, John Johnson and an Indian Woman, were married by Banns at Red River Settlement 4th November 1833 by Wm. Cockran, Assistant Chaplain of the Hon. H. B. Company, Witnesses Present: Peter Garrioch and Joseph Daniel.

Johnson, Margaret: See Baptiste DeChamp and Margaret Johnson

Johnston, Ann: See Charles Isham and Ann Johnston

Johnston, Ann: See George Sinclair and Ann Johnston

Johnston, James and Polly Anderson: No. 201, James Johnson, of Red River Settlement, and Polly Anderson of the same place, were married at Red River Settlement by Banns with consent of parties on the 31st day of May in the year 1830, by William Cockran Assist Chaplain and Missionary, In the presence of Andrew McChorister and Sarah Budd.

Johnston, John and Sally Thomas: No. 9, John Johnston and Sally Thomas, both of the Indian Settlement, were married by Banns on the 10th day of December 1835, by William Cockran, 2nd Chaplain to Hudson's Bay Compy., Witnesses: Joseph Cook and Peter Corrigal.

Hudson Bay Company Marriages 1820-1851

Johnston, William and Elisabeth Budd: No. 428, William Johnston, of Red River Settlement, and Elisabeth Budd of the same place, were married at Grand Rapids, by banns, with consent of parties this Fourth of March In the year One Thousand Eight Hundred and Forty, By me William Cochran Asst. Chaplain to the H.H.B. Company. This marriage was Solemnized between us William Johnston (his X mark) and Elisabeth Budd (her X mark), In the presence of James Neshaw and George Sinclair.

Johnstone, Donald and Nancy Daniel: No. 224, Donald Johnstone and Nancy Daniel, both of Red River Settlement, were married by Banns with consent of Parties on the 29th Day of November 1831, by William Cockran, Assistant Chaplain to the Honble Hudson's Bay Company, Witnesses Present: William Kennedy Junr and Henry Budd.

Johnstone, Jane: See George Robison and Jane Johnstone

Johnstone, Jane: See William Todd and Jane Johnstone

Jones, Catherine: See Alexander McChorister and Catherine Jones

Jordan, Hector and Janet Matheson: No. 402, Hector Jordan, bachelor, Red River Settlement, and Jane Mowat, spinster, of the same place, were married at the Upper Church, by banns, with consent of Parents, this 25th day of March, in the year of our Lord, 1847, by me, John Macallum, Solemnized between us Hector Jordan and Janet Matheson (her mark X), In the presence of Robert Sutherland and Samuel Prictchard.

Kegror, Michael and Jane: No. 115, March 2, 1826, Michael Kegror [?], of [..?..] Germany, and Jane Kegror [?], of the same place, were married by Banns with consent of parents and Parties at the Red River Settlement by David T. Jones, Chaplain to the Hon. H. Bay Company, In presence of Felix Miller and Peter Rindisbacher.

Keith, Mary: See Thomas Taylor and Mary Keith

Kennedy, Adam and Betsy Budd: No. 384, Adam Kennedy, of Red River Settlement and Betsy Budd of the same place, were married by Banns with mutual consent on the sixth day of March 1838, by William Cochran 2nd Chaplain to the Honble Hudson's Bay Company, Witnesses: Philip Kennedy and Frederick Bird.

Kennedy, Isabella: See George Setter and Isabella Kennedy

Kennedy, Mary: See Thomas Isbister and Mary Kennedy

Kennedy, Philip and Jessy McKenzie: No. 390, Philip Kennedy, of the Red River Settlement and Jessy McKenzie of the same place, were married by Banns with consent of parents on the 28th day of June in the year 1838, by David T. Jones Chaplain to the Honble Hudson's Bay Company, Witnesses: John Loyd and Elen Spence.

Hudson Bay Company Marriages 1820-1851

Keplin, Peter and Azgelick Berston: No. 155, Peter Keplin, of The Red River Settlement, and Azgelick Berston, widow, of the same place, were married in the Rapids Church by License, with consent of Parties, this Third Day of December in the year one Thousand eight hundred and forty Six by me Robert James Missionary. This marriage was Solemnized between us: Peter (his X mark) Keplin and Azelick (her X mark) Berston, In the Presence of Thomas (his mark) Anderson and Catherine (her mark) Anderson.

Kepling, Margaret: See John Lyons and Margaret Kepling

Kepling, Maria: See John Monuenie and Maria Kepling

Keppling, Edward and Nancy: No. 299, Edward Keppling, A Half Breed of Red River, and Nancy, a native woman of the same place, were married at Red River on the 3rd day of June 1835, by Wm. Cockran Assist. Chaplain to the Hon. Hudson's Bay Comp., Witnesses: John James Smith and Catherine Cook.

Kipling, Jane: See Thomas Fidler and Jane Kipling

Kipling, Margaret: See Samuel Favel and Margaret Kipling

Kipling, Susanna: See John Fidler and Susanna Kipling

Kippling, John and Mary: No. 327, John Kippling and Mary, a native woman, were married by Banns with consent of parties on the 28th December1836, by William Cochran 2nd Chaplain to the Hon. Hudson's Bay Company, Witnesses: Joseph Cook and Timothy Bear.

Kippling, Thomas and Sophy: No. 198, Thomas Kippling, of the Red River Settlement, and Sophy an Indian woman, of the same place, were married in St.Andrews Church with consent of parties this Twenty seventh day of October in the year one Thousand Eight hundred and fifty, By me, Robert James Missionary. This marriage was Solemnized between us Thomas Kippling (by mark X) and Sophy (by mark X), In the presence of George Calder (by mark X) and Thomas Lyons (by mark X).

Kirkness, John and Elizabeth Cook: No. __, John Kirkness, of the Red River Settlement, and Elizabeth Cook of the same place, were married at the Upper Church by Banns, with consent of Parents, on the 17th day of January in the year 1844, by me, Abraham Cowley, Missionary, Solemnized between us John Kirkness and Elizabeth Cook, Witnesses: Joseph Smith and Robert Spence.

Kirkness, Mary: William Birston and Mary Kirkness

Kirton, Joseph and Catharine Lyons: No. __, Joseph Kirton, Widower, of Red River Settlement, and Catharine Lyons, widow, of the same place, were married in the Upper Church, by special license and with consent of parties, this sixteenth day of November, in the year of our Lord, one thousand eight hundred and forty Seven, By me, Wm. Cochran. This marriage was Solemnized between us Joseph Kirton and Catharine Lyons, In the presence of Catharine Cunningham and James Franks.

Knechler, Salome: See John Daniel Tessot and Salome Knechler

Knight, Charlotte: See Thomas Halcro and Charlotte Knight

Knight, James and Elizabeth Heywood: No. 403, James Knight of Red River Settlement and Elizabeth Heywood of the same place were married at the Grand Rapids R.R.S. by banns with consent of Parents and Parties This sixth Day of December, In the year one thousand eight hundred and Thirty eight, By me Wm. Cochran Asst. Chaplain to the H.H.B. Company. This marriage was solemnized between us James (his X mark) Knight and Elizabeth Heywood, In the presence of Thomas Lambier and James Sandison.

Knight, James and Sophia Hallett: No. 90, James Knight and Sophia Hallett were married at the Red River Settlement by Banns, on the 11th day of April 1825, by me, David T. Jones, Asst. Chaplain, In presence of James Spence and George Harbidge.

Knight, Maria: See John Harper and Maria Knight

Knight, William and Margarret Cummings: No. 145, William Knight, of The Red River Settlement, and Margarret Cummings, of The same place, were married at the Grand Rapids, by Banns, with consent of Parents and parties, this Twelfth Day of February in the year One thousand eight hundred and Forty Six, By me, Wm. Cochran Chaplain to the H. H. B. Company. This marriage was solemnized between us: William Knight (by mark X), Margarret Cumnings (by mark X), In the presence of Rodk. Sutherland and James McKay.

Knipe, Edward and Anne Matheson: No. 415, Edward Knipe, of Royal Artillery Garrison Upper Fort, and Anne Matheson, of the Red River Settlement, were married at the Upper Church, by Special License, with consent of Parents and Parties this Thirty First day of July in the year of our Lord, one Thousand Eight Hundred and Forty Eight, by me, Wm. Cochrane, Chaplain to the H. H. B. C. Solemnized between us E. Knipe and Anne Matheson, In the presence of Angus Matheson and Catherine Matheson.

L'Eunay, Susette: See Andrew Spence and Susette L'Eunay

Lajourmoniere, Lisset: See George Saunderson and Lisset Lajoumoniere

Lambair, Jane: See Otwain De Shawrumn and Jane Lambair

Lambere, Michael and Peggy a halfbreed Woman: No. 13, Michael Lambere, of Beaver Creek and Margaret a halfbreed Woman of the same place were married at Beaver Creek this Twenty-ninth Day of January in the Year One thousand eight hundred and Twenty-One, By me John West Chaplain, This Marriage was solemnized between us Michael Lamere (x his mark) and Peggy (x her mark)m In the Presence of Alexr Robertson and George Setter.

Lambert, Mary: See James Tait and Mary Lumbere

Lambert, Michael: See Michael Lambere

Hudson Bay Company Marriages 1820-1851

Lambier, John and Ann Ishim: No. 164, James Lambier, of the Red River Settlement, and Ann Ishim, of the same place, were married in the Rapids Church by Banns and with consent of parties this ninth Day of December in the year One Thousand Eight Hundred Forty Seven by me Robert James Missionary. This marriage was solemnized between us James Lambier and Ann Ishim (her mark X), In the presence of William Hodgson and John Hodgson.

Lambier, Thomas and Fanny Ducharm: No. 163, Thomas Lambier, of the Red River Settlement, and Fanny Ducharm, of the same place, were married in the Rapids Church, by Banns, and with consent of parties, this ninth Day of December in the year One Thousand Eight Hundred Forty Seven by me Robert James Missionary. This marriage was solemnized between us Thomas Lambier and Fanny Ducharm (her mark X), In the presence of Andrew Mowat and John Setter.

Lane, Richard and Mary McDermot: No. _), Richard Lane, Clerk, Honble Hudson't Bay Company, and Mary McDermot, Red River Settlement were married, at the Upper Church, by special license, with consent of parties, this Thirteenth day of June, in the year of our Lord One Thousand Eight-Hundred and Forty Six, by me John Macallum, Solemnized between us: Richard Lane and Mary McDermot, In the presence of John Black and Andrew McDermot.

Lapoint, Marie: See Joseph Beauchamp and Marie Lapoint

LaRoque, Teresa: See Francis Monjeunere and Teresa LaRoque

Laurain, Francois: See Joshua Halcro and Francois Laurain

Lavallee, Lizette: See John Aimable MacKay and Lizette Lavallee

Lawson, Thomas and Mary Beck: No. 388, Thomas Lawson, an Englishman, now residing at Red River Settlement, and Mary Beck, resident of the same place, were married by mutual consent of parties on the 19th day of March in the year 1838, by David T. Jones Chaplain to the Honble Hudson's Bay Company, Witnesses: James Franks and Jane Emond.

Ledoux, Pierre and Susannah Short: No. 194, Pierre St.Pierre [Ledoux], White Horse Plains Settlement, Susannah Short, of the same place married at Red River Settlement on the 8th day of February (1830) Banns with consent of parties by David Jones Chaplain, In the presence of James Vollar and Donald Johnstone.

Leith, William and Elizabeth Spence: No. 114, February 20, 1826, William Leith, of Red River, and Elizabeth Spence, of the same place, were married by Banns with consent of parties at Red River Settlement by William Cockran Assistant Chaplain, In presence of Joseph Bird and Mr. John Bunn.

Lewes, Fanny Lee: See James Ballenden and Fanny Lee Lewes

Lewes, Mary: See Jean Baptiste Burau and Mary Lewes

Lewis, Margaret: See James Spence and Margaret Lewis

Lilley, Daniel and Mary Ann Richards: No. 442, Daniel Lilley, of Red River Settlement, and Mary Ann Richards, of the same place, were married at the Middle Church, by banns, with consent of Parties this Seventeenth day of December in the year 1840 By me William Cochran Asst. Chaplain to the H.H.B. Company. Solemnized between us Daniel Lilley and Mary Ann Richards (by X mark), In the presence of John Pritchard and Thos. Thomas.

Linklater, Andrew and Catherine Longmore: No. 204, Andrew Linklater of Red River settlement and Catherine Longmore of the same place were married at Red River Church by Banns this 22nd day of June 1830 by D. T. Jones in the presence of William Sutherland and William Taylor.

Linklater, Catherine: See Simon Thomas and Catherine Linklater

Linklater, Elizabeth: See James Fidler and Elizabeth Linklater

Linklater, Hugh and Charlotte Corrigal: No. 101, Hugh Linklater, of Red River Settlement, and Charlotte Corrigal, of the same place, were married at the Grand Rapids by Banns with Consent of Parties this Sixth day of December in the year One thousand eight hundred and Forty One, by me Wm. Cochran Chaplain to the Hon. H. B. Company. This marriage was solemnized between us Hugh Linklater (by mark X) and Charlotte Corrigal (by mark X), In the presence of Malcome Cumming and George Davis.

Linklater, John and Elizabeth Saunders: No. 193, John Linklater, a half breed of Albany, southern Dept. and Elizabeth Saunders of the same place, were married at Red River by Banns this fourth day of Feb. 1830 by David T. Jones Chaplain to the Hon Hudson's Bay Co. in the presence of William Sanderson and Charles Fidler.

Linklater, John and Ellen Peebles: No. 202, John Linklater, of the Parish of St.Andrews Red River Settlement, and Ellen Peebles, of the same place, were married in St.Andrews Church by banns and with consent of parties this nineteenth day of December in the year one Thousand Eight hundred and fifty, By me, Robert James Missionary. This marriage was Solemnized between us John Linklater and Ellen Peebles (by mark X), In the presence of Archibald Johnson and Sutherland Peebles (by mark X).

Linklater, Margaret: See William Daniel and Margaret Linklater

Lions, Thomas and Charlotte Pruden: No. 157, Thomas Lions, of the Red River Settlement, and Charlotte Pruden, of the Same place, were married in the Rapids Church, by Banns, with consent of Parties This Tenth Day of December the year One Thousand Eight Hundred and Forty Six, By me, Robert James Missionary. This marriage was Solemnized between us: Thomas Lions (his mark X) and Charlotte Pruden (her mark X), In the presence of William Dahall and Thomas Folster (his mark X).

Lisk, William and Mary Cook: No. 207, William Lisk [sic] of Red River Settlement and Mary Cook of the same place were married at Red River Church on the 18th day of November 1830, by David T. Jones Chaplain to the Honble H.B.C., Witnesses Present: James Birston and William Flett.

Livingston, Catherine: See John McLean and Catherine Livingston

Livingstone, Anne: See Donald Sutherland and Anne Livingstone

Hudson Bay Company Marriages 1820-1851

Livingstone, Hugh and Isabella Rose: No. 203, Hugh Livingstone, of Red River Settlement, and Isabella Rose, of the same place, were married at Red River Settlement by Banns with mutual consent on the 3rd day of June in the year 1830, by David T. Jones,k Chaplain to the Hon. Hudson's Bay, In the presence of Hugh Rose and John Livingstone.

Livingstone, Isabella: See Angus Matheson and Isabella Livingstone

Livingstone, John and Sophia McDonell: No. 285, John Livingstone, of Red River SEttlement, and Sophie McDonell, now of the same place, were married by Banns on the 18th day of December 1834, By D. T. Jones, Chaplain to the Honble. H. B. Company, Witnesses: Neil Livingstone and Morrison McBeath.

Livingstone, Mary: See Roderick MacBeath and Mary Livingstone

Livingstone, Neil and Catherine Manson: No. 295, Neil Livingstone of Red River Settlement, and Catherine Manson of the same place, were married by Banns at Red River Church on the 19th day of February in the year 1835, by David T. Jones, Chaplain to The Honble. Hudson's Bay Company, Witnesses: Dond. Murray and Morrison McBeath.

Logan, Anne: See Neil McDonald and Anne Logan

Logan, Elizabeth: See William Sutherland and Elizabeth Logan

Logan, Robert and Mary a Sauteaux Indian Woman: No. 8, Robert Logan, a Principal Settler of the Red River Colony and Mary, a Sauteueax of the same place were married at Red River Settlement this Thirteenth Day of January in the Year One thousand eight hundred and Twenty-One, By me John West Chaplain, This Marriage was solemnized between us Robert Logan and Mary (x her mark), In the Presence of Alexr MacDonell and Wm. Laidlaw.

Logan, Robert and Mrs. Sarah Ingham: No. 417, Robert Logan Esqr, Widower of Red River Settlement and Mrs. Sarah Ingham, widow of the same place, were married at Point Douglas, with consent of parties this Twenty ninth Day of July In the year One Thousand Eight Hundred and Thirty nine, By me William Cochran Asst. Chaplain to the H.H.B. Company. This marriage was Solemnized between us Robert Logan and Sarah Ingham, In the presence of Dun Finlayson and Alex Rod. McLeod.

Logan, Thomas and Margaret Cummings: No. 254, Thomas Logan and Margaret Cummings were married by Banns at Red River Settlement 21st February 1833, By The Revd. William Cockran, Assist. Chaplain the Honble. Hudson's Bay Company, Witnesses Present: James McMillan and Joseph Charles.

Logan, Thomas and Mary Anne Dease: No. 334, Thomas Logan and Mary Anne Dease were married at Red River Settlement by Banns with mutual consent on the 7th day of February 1837, by David T. Jones, Chaplain to the Honble. Hudson's Bay Company, Witnesses: Francis M. Dease and Neil MacDonald.

Longmore, Catherine: See Andrew Linklater and Catherine Longmore

Louis, James and Barbara Gibson: No. 144, James Louis, A Negro Half Breed, of Red River, and Barbara Gibson, A Half Breed, of the same place, were married at Red River Church, by Banns with mutual consent on the 18th day of December 1827 by David T. Jones Chaplain and Missionary, Present at the ceremony: John Park and James Whitequay.

Louis, James and Isabella Spense: No. 2, James Louis and Isabella Spense, both of Red River Settlement, were married by Banns with consent of parties, on the 16th day of November in the year 1835, by William Cockran Asst. Chaplain Hon. H.B. Co., Witnesses present: James Settee and Andrew Spense.

Louis, Margaret: See James Sandison and Margaret Louis

Lowman, Mary Emily: See Roderick Sutherland and Mary Emily Lowman

Lowman, Mary: See James Bird

Lyons, Catharine: See Joseph Kirton and Catharine Lyons

Lyons, James and Catherine Cook: No. 26, James Lyons and Catherine Cook, of Red River Settlement, were married by Banns on the 17th day of March 1836, by Wm. Cockran, 2nd Chaplain to The Hon. H. B. Co., Witnesses: Anne Cockran and Margaret Garrioch.

Lyons, John and Margaret Gibson: No. 372, John Lyons, of Red River Settlement, and Margaret Gibson, of the same place, were married by Banns with consent of parents and parties, on the 7th day of December in the year 1837, by William Cochran, 2nd Chaplain to the Hon. Hudson's Bay Company, Witnesses: James Sutherland and John Sutherland.

Lyons, John and Margaret Kepling: No. 142, John Lyons, a Jewish Half Breed, and Margaret Kepling, a H. Breed of Red River, were married by Banns at the Rapids of Red River on the 18th day of December 1827, Wm. Cockran, Asst. Chaplain, Witnesses present: Donald Gunn, Wm. R. Smith.

Lyons, Mary: See Charles Cook and Mary Lyons

Lyons, Nancy: See Magnus Birston and Nancy Lyons

Macallum, John and Elizabeth Charles: No. 22, John Macallum of Fortron Scotland and Elizabeth Charles of Red River Colony, were married by Banns with consent of parents and parties on the 16th day of February in the year 1836, by David T. Jones, Chaplain to The Honble. H. B. Compy., Witnesses: Alexander Christie, Thos. Simpson, and John Ballenden.

MacBeath, Robert and Mary MacLean: No. 228, Robert MacBeath and Mary MacLean both of Red River Settlement were married by Banns with Consent of Parties this 19th day of January by David T. Jones Chaplain to the Honble Hudson's Bay Company, Witnesses Present: John Pritchard and Wm. Robt. Smith

Hudson Bay Company Marriages 1820-1851

MacBeath, Roderick and Mary Livingstone: No. 231, Roderick MacBeath and Mary Livingstone, both of Red River Settlement, were married by Banns with consent of Parties on the159th Day of February 1832, by William Cockran Assistant Chaplain to the Honble. Hudson's Bay Company, Witnesses Present: Donald Livingstone and Robert MacBeath.

Macdonald, John and Sarah Swaine: No. 94, John Macdonald and Sarah Swaine were married by Banns at the Red River Settlement on the 12th day of July 1825 by me, David T. Jones Assistant Chaplain, In presence of Wm Garrioch and Joseph Cook.

Macdonald, Kenneth and Elizabeth Calder: No. 102, October 28th 1825, Kenneth Macdonald, Red River Settlement and Elizabeth Calder, of the same place, were married at Red River Settlement by Banns with consent of parties by David T. Jones Chaplain to the Thon. Hudson's Bay Company, In present of William Garrioch, Schoolmaster and James Sandison, Settler.

Mackay, Charles and Letitia Bird: No. 130, Charles Mackay, a H. Breed of River River, and Letitia Bird, a H. Breed of the same place were married at Red River Settlement by Bans with consent of parents and parties on 2 Oct 1827 by David T. Jones Chaplain, Present: James Bird and Robert ... ?.

MacKay, Christy: See Alexander MacLean and Christy MacKay

Mackay, Dorothea: See Joseph Bremner and Dorothea Mackay

Mackay, Jerry and Margaret Halcro: No. 426, Jerry Mackay, of the Indian Settlement, and Margaret Halcro of the same place, were married at the Grand Rapids, by banns, with consent of parents this second day of January In the year One Thousand Eight Hundred and Forty, By me William Cochran Asst. Chaplain to the H.H.B. Company. This marriage was Solemnized between us Jerry Mackay (his X mark) and Margaret Halcro (her X mark), In the presence of Joseph Halcro and Mary Buxton.

MacKay, John Aimable MacKay and Lizette Lavallee: No. 236, John Aimable MacKay, Laborer, ... and Lizette Lavallee, were married by Banns with consent of Parties this 12th Day of March 1832, by David T. Jones Chaplain to the Honble. Hudsons Bay Company, Witnesses Present: W. Robt Smith and Harriette [?].
MacKay, Mary: See John Bird and Mary MacKay

Mackenzie, Donald and Adelgone Humbert Droz: No. 96, Donald Mackenzie, of The Hudsons Bay Company's Service and Adelgonde Humbert Droz of Red River Settlement were married by consent of parties on 18 August 1825 by David T. Jones, Chaplain to The Hudson's Bay Company, In the presence of Robert Logan and Francis Heron, Clerk of the store named Fort Garry.

MacKie, Sophia: See Thomas Cameron and Sophia MacKie

MacLean, Alexander and Christy MacKay: No. 233, Alexander MacLean and Christy MacKay, both of Red River Settlement, were married by Banns with consent of Parties this 17th Day of February 1832, by D. T. Jones, Chaplain to the Honble. Hudsons Bay Company, Witnesses Present: Robert ...

MacLean, Mary: See Robert MacBeath and Mary MacLean

Hudson Bay Company Marriages 1820-1851

Macnab, John and Margaret Saunders: No. 141, John Macnab, A Half Breed Settler, and Margaret Saunders, A Half Breed too, were married at the Rapids of Red River, by Banns with mutual consent on the 18th of December 1827 by Wm. Cockran Assistant Chaplain, Witnesses present: Donald Gunn and Wm. R. Smith.

Macnab, Thomas and Mary: No. 140, Thos. Macnab, A Half Breed Settler of the Red River Colony and Mary, Seaulteaux Indian woman; were married by Banns with mutual consent, at the Rapids of Man, on the 10th day of December 1827 by Wm. Cockran Asst Chaplain, Present at the Ceremonies: Wm. R. Smith, Donald Gunn.

Macrae, George and Ellen Sutherland: No. 3, George Macrae of the Red River Colony and Ellen Sutherland of the same place were married at Fort Douglas by Banns this Twenty fourth Day of November in the year One thousand eight hundred and Twenty, By me John West Chaplain, This Marriage was solemnized between us George Mckrae (signed) and Ellen Sutherland (x her mark), In the Presence of Wm. Laidlaw and George Harbidge.

Manson, Catherine: See Neil Livingstone and Catherine Manson

Marchand, Hazelique: See William Birston and Hazelique Marchand

Marchant, Augustine: See Antoine Paquet and Augustine Marchant

Marchant, Justine: See Justine Marchant and Antoine Baen

Martineau, Mary: See Andrew Dennet and Mary Martinois

Mason, Rev. William and Sophia Thomas: No. 367, The Revd. William Mason of the Wesleyan Missionary Society Lately stationed in the Lac La Pluie District, and Sophia Thomas of Red River Settlement, were married, near the Middle Church by mutual consent of parties, on the 10th day of August in the year 1843, by me, William Cochran Chaplain to the H. H. B. C. Solemnized between us William Mason and Sophia Thomas, Witnesses: John McCallum and Dun. Finlayson.

Matheson, Angus and Isabella Livingstone: No. 325, Angus Matheson and Isabella Livingstone were married at Red River Settlement with consent of parties, on the 22nd December in the year 1836, by William Cochran 2nd Chaplain to the Hon. Hudson's Bay Company, Witnesses: Angus Matheson and John Polson. Matheson, Angus and Margaret Gunn: No. 286, Angus Matheson, of Red River Settlement, and Margaret Gunn, of the same place, were married at Red River Settlement by Banns with consent of parties, on the 18th day of December 1834, By D. T. Jones, Chaplain to the Honble. H. B. Company, Witnesses: Geo. Matheson and Morrison McBeath.

Matheson, Anne: See Donald Sutherland and Anne Matheson

Matheson, Anne: See Edward Knipe and Anne Matheson

Matheson, Catherine: See John Sutherland and Catherine Matheson

Hudson Bay Company Marriages 1820-1851

Matheson, Donald and Barbara Frazer: No. 399, Donald Matheson of the Red River Settlement and Barbara Frazer of the same place were married at the Middle Church RRS by banns with consent of Parents and Parties This first day of November, In the year one thousand eight hundred and thirty eight, By me Wm. Cochran Asst. Chaplain to the H. H. B. Company. This marriage was solemnized between us Donald Matheson and Barbara (her X mark) Frazer, In the presence of W. R. Smith and James Tate.

Matheson, Hugh and Christy Matheson: No. 373, Hugh Matheson, of Red River Settlement, and Christy Matheson, of the same place, were married by Banns with consent of parties and parents, on the 14th day of December in the year 1837, by David T. Jones, Chaplain to the Hon. Hudson's Bay Company, Witnesses: Angus Matheson and John Polson.

Matheson, Hugh and Letitia Pritchard: No. __, Hugh Matheson, bachelor, of Red River Settlement, and Letitia Pritchard, Spinster, of the same place, were married in the Upper Church, by special license and with consent of parties, this ninth day of December, in the year of our Lord, one thousand eight hundred and forty Seven, By me, Wm. Cochran. This marriage was Solemnized between us Hugh Matheson and Letita Pritchard, In the presence of Samuel Matheson and Archibald Pritchard.

Matheson, Hugh and Margaret Ross: No. 411, Hugh Matheson of Red River Settlement and Margaret Ross of the same place were married at the Colony Garden R.R.S. by banns with the consent of Parents and Parties This seventh Day of March In the year one thousand eight hundred and thirty eight [nine?] By me Wm. Cochran Asst Chaplain to the H.H.B. Company. This marriage was solemnized between us Hugh Matheson and Margaret Ross, In the presence of Alexander Ross and Francis McKeile Dease.

Matheson, James and Jane Matheson: No. 89, James Matheson and Jane Matheson were married at Red River Settlement by Banns, on the 25th day of January 1825, by me, David T. Jones, Assistant Chaplain, In presence of George Flett, George Harbidge.

Matheson, James and Margaret Sutherland: No. 214, James Matheson of Red River Settlement and Margaret Sutherland of the same place were married at Red River Church on the 10 day of March 1831 by David T. Jones Chaplain to the Honourable Hudsons Bay Company, Witnesses Present: John Mathesson and George Munro.

Matheson, Jane: See James Matheson and Jane Matheson

Matheson, Jane: See John Fraser and Jane Matheson

Matheson, Janet: See Donald Bannerman and Janet Matheson

Matheson, Janet: See Hector Jordan and Janet Matheson

Matheson, Jannet: See John Pritchard and Jannet Matheson

Hudson Bay Company Marriages 1820-1851

Matheson, John and Anne Polson: No. 60, John Matheson, of the Red River Colony, and Anne Polson of the Same place were married at the Church Mission House with Consent of Parents by Banns this Fifth day of June in the Year One thousand eight hundred and Twenty three, By me, John West, Chaplain. This Marriage was solemnized between us John Mathison and Ann Polson (x her mark), In the Presence of Alexr Polson and George Harbidge.

Matheson, John and Catherine Pritchard: No. 441, John Matheson, of Red River Settlement, and Catherine Pritchard, of the same place, were married, by banns at the Middle Church with consent of Parents and Parties this Seventeenth day of December in the year 1840 By me William Cochran Asst. Chaplain to the H.H.B. Company. Solemnized between us John Matheson and Catherine Pritchard, In the presence of John Pritchard and Thos. Thomas.

McBeath, Adam and Mary McKenzie: No. 437, Adam McBeath, of McKenzie River District, and Mary McKenzie, of the same place, were married at Fort Simpson with consent of Parties this Twenty fifth day of May in the year 1838 By me M. McPherson Magistrate, Solemnized between us Adam McBeath and Mary McKenzie, In the presence of Wm. Johnstone and John Sandison.

McBeath, Christiana: See Alexander Sutherland and Christiana McBeath

McBeath, George and Catherine Sutherland: No. 71, December 23, 1823, George McBeath and Catherine Sutherland, Witnesses: John Sutherland, Donald Murray. Marriages celebrated at the Red River Colony from October 1823 to July 1824 by me, David T. Jones 2nd Chaplain.

McBeath, Morrison and Isabella Gunn: No. 3, Morrison McBeath and Isabella Gunn, both Scotch Settlers of Red River Settlement, were married by Banns, with consent of parents and parties on the 26th day of November 1835, by David T. Jones Chaplain to The Hon. H. B. Co., Witnesses: Adam McBeath and William Gunn.

McChorister, Alexander and Catherine Jones: No. 136, Alexander McChorister, of ... Hudson's Bay, and Catherine Jones of the same place were married at the Red River Colony, with consent of parties, by Banns, on the 27th day of November 1827, D. T. Jones Chaplain to the H. H. B. Company, Present at the ceremony: Donald Gunn and John McDonald.

McChorister, Andrew and Mary Donald: No. 294, Andrew McChorister, of Red River Settlement, and Mary Donald of the same place, were married by Banns at Red River Settlement on the 13th day of February in the year 1835, by Wm. Cockran 2nd Chaplain to the Honble. Hudson's Bay Compy., Witnesses: Wm. Donald and Philip Kennedy.

McCorrister, Catherine: See Alexander McKay and Catherine McCorrister

McCorrister, Henry and Maria Tate: No. _, Henry Macorrister, Bachelor, of Red River Settlement and Maria Tate Spinster of the same place, were married, in the Upper Church, by Banns with consent of Parents, on the 30th day of November in the yare 1843, by Abraham Cowley, Missionary...

Hudson Bay Company Marriages 1820-1851

McCorrister, James and Elizabeth McNab: No. 422, James McCorrister, widower, Red River Settlement, and Elizabeth McNab, of the same place, were married at the Upper Church, by Banns, with consent of Parties, this 1st Feb 1849, by me, Wm. Cochran, Chaplain to the H. H. B. Co., Solemnized between us James McCorrister and Elizabeth McNab, In the presence of James Johnston and W. Sandison.

McCorrister, John and Ann Donald: No. 195, John McCorrister, of the Parish of St.Andrew's Red River Settlement, and Ann Donald, of the same place, were married in St.Andrews Church by Banns and with consent of parties this Twenty first day of February in the year one Thousand Eight hundred and fifty, By me, Robert James Missionary. This marriage was Solemnized between us John McCorrister (by mark X) and Ann Donald (by mark X), In the presence of John Gunn and James McCorrister.

McDermot, Catherine: See Thomas Truthwair and Catherine McDermot

McDermot, Mary: See Richard Lane and Mary McDermot

McDermot, Mary: See Thomas Bird and Mary McDermot

McDonald, Alexander and Elizabeth Robillard: No. 206, Alexander MacDonald, of the parish of St.Andrews Red River Settlement, and Elizabeth Robillard, of the same place, were married in St.Andrews Church by banns \ with consent of parties this Twelfth day of June in the year one Thousand Eight hundred and fifty one, By me, John Chapman. This marriage was Solemnized between us Alexander McDonald (by mark X) and Elizabeth Robeyor (x), In the presence of Cuthbert Cummings and Joseph Tait.

McDonald, Archibald and Jane: No. 300, Archibald McDonald, Chief Trader, Hudson's Bay Company's Service and Jane, a Half -Caste Native, were married by mutual consent at Red River Settlement on the 9th day of June in the year 1835, by Wm. Cockran, 2nd Chaplain to The Hon. Hudson's Bay Company, Witnesses: David T. Jones, Chaplain, Alex. Christie Chief Factor, Dn. Finlayson Chief Factor.

McDonald, Donald and Janet Bethune: No. 74, February 5th, 1824, Donald McDonald and Janet Bethune, Witnesses: Donald McDonald, Benjamin Gunn. Marriages celebrated at the Red River Colony from October 1823 to July 1824 by me, David T. Jones 2nd Chaplain.

McDonald, Donald and Jean Boodry: No. 431, Donald McDonald, of Red River Settlement, and Jean Boodry of the same place, were married at Grand Rapids, by banns, with consent of parties this seventeenth Day of March In the year One Thousand Eight Hundred and Forty, By me William Cochran Asst. Chaplain to the H.H.B. Company. This marriage was Solemnized between us Donald McDonald and Jean Boodry (her X mark), In the presence of Thomas Firth and Donald Gunn.

McDonald, Donald and Nancy Ferguson: Donald McDonald, married 24 Mar 1829, Nancy Ferguson. (Denney)

McDonald, Flora: See John Folster and Flora McDonald

McDonald, Neil and Anne Logan: No. 127, Neil McDoanld, of the Island of Islay Scotland, and Anne Logan, of the Red River Settlement, were married by Banns at Red River Settlement, on the 29th day of March 1827, by David T. Jones Chaplain, In the presence of Alexander McDonald and Duncan Finlayson.

Hudson Bay Company Marriages 1820-1851

McDonald, William and Catharine Gunn: No. 358, William McDonald, of Red River Settlement, and Catharine Gunn, of the same place, were married at the Upper Church by Banns with Consent of Parties this Seventh day of October in the year One thousand eight hundred and Forty One, by me Wm. Cochran Chaplain to the Hon. H. B. Company. This marriage was solemnized between us William McDonald and Catharine Gunn (by mark X), In the presence of John Macallum and William Brown.

McDonald, William and Margarret Mowat: No. 136, William McDonald, of The Red River Settlement, and Margarret Mowat, of the same place, were married at the Grand Rapids, by Banns, with consent of Parents and parties, this Ninth Day of January in the year One thousand eight hundred forty five By me Wm. Cochran Chaplain to the H. H. B. Company. This marriage was Solemnized between us: William McDonald (by mark X), Margarret Mowat (by mark X), In the presence of Thomas Truthwaite and James Gunn.

McDonell, Sophia: See John Livingstone and Sophia McDonell

McIntosh, William and Sarah Gladue: No. 35, William McIntosh, Chief Factor Hon ble. Hudsons Company. Service and Sarah Gladue, his reputed wife, were married on the 28th day of June 1836, by David T. Jones, Chapln. to The Hon. H. B. Company, Witnesses: Alexander Christie and John Lloyd.

McIver, Allan and Elizabeth Beads: No. 170, Allan McIver, of Beaver Creek in the H. H. B. Company Service, and Elizabeth Beads, of the same place, were married in the Rapids Church, by License and with consent of parties, this Fifth Day of June in the year, one thousand eight Hundred and Forty Eight, By me, Robert James Missionary. This marriage was Solemnized between us Allan McIver and Elizabeth Beads, In the presence of Archibald Johnston and James Forbister.

McKay, Alexander and Catherine McCorrister: No. 187, Alexander McKay, of Red River Settlement, and Catherine McCorrister, of the same place, were married in the Rapid's Church by Banns and with consent of Parties this Twenty six day of July in the year One Thousand eight Hundred and forty nine, by me, Robert James Missionary. This marriage was Solemnized between us Alexander McKay (by mark X) and Catherine McCorrister (by mark X), In the presence of John Gunn and James Gunn.

McKay, James and Margaret Gladu: No. 432, James McKay, of Red River Settlement, and Margaret Glandu of the same place, were married at Grand Rapids, by banns, with consent of parties this seventeenth Day of March In the year One Thousand Eight Hundred and Forty, By me William Cochran Asst. Chaplain to the H.H.B. Company. This marriage was Solemnized between us James McKay and Margaret Glanu (her X mark), In the presence of Thomas Firth and Donald McDonald.

McKay, Jenott: See Alexander Bannerman and Jenott McKay

McKay, John and Sarah Tate: No. 250, John McKay, a Native Indian, and Sarah Tate, of the same caste, were married by banns at Red River Settlement 14 December 1832, By David T. Jones, Chaplain to the Honble. Hudson's Bay Company, Witnesses Present: Robert Sanderson and Homiey [?].

Hudson Bay Company Marriages 1820-1851

McKay, John Richards and Harriett Ballenden: No. 9, John Richards Mackay, of Brandon House and Harriett Ballenden of the same place were married at Brandon House this Twenty first Day of January in the Year One thousand eight hundred and Twenty-One, By me John West Chaplain, This Marriage was solemnized between us John Richards McKay and Harriette Ballenden, In the Presence of James Inkster and John Matheson.

McKay, Madelaine: See Giffith Daniel and Madelaine McKay

McKay, Mary: See Wm. Sinclair and Mary McKay

McKay, Selkirk and Elspy: No. 360, Selkirk McKay, of Red River Settlement, and Elspy McKay, of the same place, were married at the Upper Church by Banns with Consent of Parents and Parties this Third day of March in the year One thousand eight hundred and Forty One, by me Wm. Cochran Chaplain to the Hon. H. B. Company. This marriage was solemnized between us Selkirk McKay and Elspy McKay, In the presence of James Cunningham and John Sutherland.

McKay, William and Julia Chalifoux: No. 122, William McKay, a native of North West Territories and Julia Chalifoux, same place, were married with consent of parties, at Norway House, on the 13th day of August 1826, by David T. Jones Chaplain, In the Presence of John Dougald Cameron and John McLeod.
McKenzie, Annabella: See John Clarke Spence and Annabella McKenzie

McKenzie, Donald and Matilda Bruce: No. 316, Donald McKenzie and Matilda Bruce, were married at Red River Settlement by consent of pareties on the 17th day of October in the year 1836, by William Cockran, 2nd Chaplain to the Honble. Hudson's Bay Compy., Witnesses: Thomas Simpson and Wm. Mactavish.

McKenzie, Isabella: See Cornelius Pruden and Isabella McKenzie

McKenzie, James and Nancy Setter: No. 185, James McKenzie, of Red River Settlement, and Nancy Setter, of the same place, were married in the Rapid's Church by Banns and with consent of Parties this Twelfth day of July in the year One Thousand eight Hundred and forty nine, by me, Robert James Missionary. This marriage was Solemnized between us James McKenzie and Nancy Setter, In the presence of John Bruce and John Setter.

McKenzie, Jessy: See Philip Kennedy and Jessy McKenzie

McKenzie, Margaret: See Peter Garrioch and Margaret McKenzie

McKenzie, Mary: See Adam McBeath and Mary McKenzie

McKenzie, Nancy: See John Setter and Nancy McKenzie

Hudson Bay Company Marriages 1820-1851

McKenzie, Roderic and Sally Sutherland: No. 56, Roderic McKenzie of the Bas La Riviere, Chief Trader, and Sally Sutherland of the same place were married at the Fort Alexander this Twentieth Day of March in the Year One thousand Eight hundred and twenty three, By me, John West, Chaplain, This Marriage was solemnized between us Roderic McKenzie and Sally Sutherland (x her mark), In the Presence of John Bell and James Beattom.

McKnab, John and Betsy Walking Chief: No. 410, John McKnab of Red River Settlement and Betsy Walkingchief of the same place were married at the middle Church R.R.S. by banns with the consent of Parents and Parties This Twenty Fourth Day of January In the year one thousand eight hundred and thirty eight [nine?] By me Wm. Cochran Asst Chaplain to the H.H.B. Company. This marriage was solemnized between us John (his X mark) McKnab and Betsy (her X mark) Walkingchief, In the presence of George Prince and William Garrioch.

McLean, John and Catherine Livingston: No. 59, John McClean, of Red River Colony, and Catherine Livingston of the same place were married at the Church Mission House by banns this Eighth Day of April in the Year One thousand Eight hundred and twenty three, By me, John West, Chaplain. This Marriage was solemnized between us John McLean (x his mark) and Catherine Livingston (x her mark), In the Presence of Donald Livingston and Donald McDonald.

McLeod, John and Betsey Swain: No. 180, John McLeod, of Red River Settlement, and Betsey Swain, of the same place, were married at Red River Settlement by Banns with consent of parties on the 8th day of September 1829, by Wm. Cockran Asst. Chaplain and Missionary, In presence of Wm. Robert Smith and Donald Gunn.

McLeod, John and Charlotte Pruden: ** John McLeod married 19 Aug 1828 at Norway House Charlotte Pruden. (List of HBC Marriages, Joanne J. Hughes, c1977)

McLeod, Sarah: See John Ballenden and Sarah McLeod

McNab, Elizabeth: See James McCorrister and Elizabeth McNab

McNab, James and Sarah Michael: No. 20, James McNab and Sarah Michael, of Red River Colony, were married by Banns with consent of parties, on the 21st Jany. 1836, by David T. Jones, Chaplain to The Hon. H. B. Compy., Witnesses: John Swain and Baptiste Rivard.

McNab, Jane: See Robert Sanison and Jane McNab

McNab, Margaret: See William Flett and Margaret McNab

McNab, Mary: See James Bruce and Mary McNab

Merz, Henry Louis and Alice Sophie Flotooh: No. 117, Henry Louis Merz [?] of the [..?..] and Alice Sophie Flotooh of the same place, were married by Banns with consent of parties at Red River Settlement, by David T. Jones, Chaplain to the Honorable Hudsons Bay Co., Witnesses: Louis [..?..] Droz and Jacob Aophore [?].

Hudson Bay Company Marriages 1820-1851

Meyer, John and Margarette Aberlae: No. 44, Jean Meyer of the Red River Colony and Margarette Aberlae of the same place were married at Fort Garry this Second Day of May the Year One thousand eight hundred and Twenty Two, By me, John West, Chaplain, This Marriage was solemnized between us Jean Meyer and Margarette Abertae (x her mark), In the Presence of Walther de Huser and Wm. Todd.

Michael, Sarah: See James McNab and Sarah Michael

Millar, Robert and Elizabeth Setter: No. 435, Robert Millar, Servant to the H. B. Company of Swan River District, and Elizabeth Settler at the Red River Settlement, were married at the Rapids, with consent of Parents and parties this This Seventeenth Day of August In the year 1840, By me William Cochran Asst. Chaplain to the H.H.B. Company. This marriage was solemnized between us Robert Millar and Elizabeth Setter (by mark X), In the presence of Andrew Setter and James Spence.

Miller, Felix and Mary Margaretta Theya: No. 121, Felix Miller of the Canton of Zurich Switzerland and Mary Margaretta Theya of Wastsonberg, German, were married by Banns at Red River Settlement on the 19th day of July 1826, By David T. Jones Chaplain, In the presence of William Cochran and David Esson.

Monjeunere, Francis and Teresa LaRoque: No. 315, Francis Monjeunere and Teresa LaRoque, were married by Banns with consent of parties on the 22nd day of August in the year 1836 by David T. Jones, Chapln. to the Honble. H. B. Company, Witnesses: Duncan Campbell and Richard Atkinson.

Monjeunier, Francis and Mary Charlats: No. 181, Francis Monjeunier, of Red River Settlement, and Mary Charlats, of the same place, were married at Red River by Banns with consent of parties the 8th day of September in the year 1829, by Wm. Cockran Asst. Chaplain and Missionary, In presence of William Robert Smith and Donald Gunn.

Monkman, Anne: See James Whitequay and Ann Monkman

Monkman, James and Mary: No. 137. James Monkman, a Native of Yorkshire, England, and Mary, an Indian woman of Severne Factory, were married at Red River Settlement by Banns with mutual consent on the 29th day of November 1827 by Wm. Cockran Asst Chaplain of Hon H.B.Co., Present at the Ceremony: Thomas Thomas, John Bunn.

Monkman, John and Mary Richards: No. __, John Monkman, bachelor, of Red River Settlement, and Mary Richards, Spinster, of the same place, were married in the Upper Church, by special license and with consent of parties, this twenty third day of December, in the year of our Lord, one thousand eight hundred and forty Seven, By me, Wm. Cochran. This marriage was Solemnized between us John Monkman and Mary Richards, In the presence of William Whiteway and Jane Monkman.

Monkman, Joseph and Isabella Setter: No. 13, Joseph Monkman and Isabella Setter, both of Red River Settlement, were married by Banns with consent of parties, on the 30th day of December 1835, by David T. Jones, Chapln. to Honble. H. B. Company, Witnesses: Alexander Christie and Charles Bird.

Monkman, Mary: See Harry Narquay and Mary Monkman

Monnier, Marianne: See Alfred Quinche and Marianne Monnier

Hudson Bay Company Marriages 1820-1851

Monnier, Rosette: See Jacob Bender and Rosette Monnier

Monuenie, John and Maria Kepling: No. 429, John Monjenie, Widower, Red River Settlement, and Maria Kepling, Spinster, of the same place, were married, by license, at the Upper Church with consent of parties, this 4th day of Jun 1849, By me, Wm. Cochran, Chaplain to the H. H. B. Co., Solemnized between us John Monjenie and Maria Kepling, In the presence of Francis Monjenie and Catherine Kepling.

Moody, Margaret: See William Favel and Margaret Moody

Moor, Elizabeth: See John Lee Lewis Smith and Elizabeth Moor

Moore, John and Clemence Ross: No. 80, John Moore and Clemence Ross were married by Banns at Red River Settlement on the 15th of September 1824 by me, David T. Jones Asst. Chaplain, in presence of John Park, Joseph Spence.

Morasay, Frances and Jane Favel: No. 356, Frances Morasay, of Red River Settlement, and Jane Favel, of the same place, were married at the Upper Church by Banns with Consent of Parents and Parties this Twenty First day of September in the year One thousand eight hundred and Forty One, by me Wm. Cochran Chaplain to the Hon. H. B. Company. This marriage was solemnized between us Frances Morasay (by mark X) and Jane Favel (by mark X), In the presence of William Tate and William Bremner.

Morell, Jean and Sophie Aberlae: No. 42, Jean Morell of the Red River Colony and Sophie Aberlae of the same place were married at Fort Gibralter this Eighteenth Day of April the Year One thousand eight hundred and Twenty Two, By me, John West, Chaplain, This Marriage was solemnized between us Jean Morell and Sophie Aberlae (x her mark) In the Presence of Walther de Huser and Geo. Simpson.

Morris, Robert and Mary Rolfe Fouman: No. 149, Robert Morris, of The Red River Settlement, and Mary Rolfe Fouman of The same place, were married at the Rapid Church, by License with consent of parties, This Fifth Day of November in the year one Thousand Eight Hundred and forty Six, By me Robert James Missionary. This marriage was Solemnized between us Robt. Morris and Mary Rolfe Fouman, In the presence of William Sinclair and Emma James.

Morrison, Angus and Ann Cunningham: No. __, Angus Morrison, a resident of Fort Pelly, Swan River District, and Ann Cunnningham, spinster of the Red River Settlement, were married at the Upper Church, by special license, with consent of parties, this Thirteenth day of June in the year of our Lord One Thousand, Eight Hundred, and Forty Six, by me John Macdallum, Soliminzed between us: Angus Morrison and Ann Cunningham, In the presence of: James Cunningham and Neil Campbell.

Morwick, James and Sarah: No. 443, James Morwick, of Red River Settlement, and Sarah Morwick, of the same place, were married at the Rapids, with consent of Parties this Twenty Third day of December in the year 1840 By me William Cochran Asst. Chaplain to the H.H.B. Company. Solemnized between us James Morwick and Sarah Morwick (by X mark), In the presence of George Ross and Donald McDonald.

Morwick, Jane see Jane Murwick

Hudson Bay Company Marriages 1820-1851

Morwick, Jane: See James Setter and Jane Morwick

Morwick, John and Isabella Norquay: No. 107, December 13, 1825, John Morwick, a Native of Ronaldand [?], Orkneys, and Isabella Norquay of Red River Colony, were married at Red River Settlement, by Banns with consent of parties by D. T. Jones Chaplain to the Hudson's Bay Company, In presence of Thomas Thomas Esq and Mr. John Bunn.

Mowat, Adam and Jane Asham: No. 105, December 6, 1825, Adam Mowat, a native of Okney, North Britain, and Jane Asham, of Red River Settlement, were married at Red River Colony by Banns, with consent of parties by David T. Jones, Chaplain to the Hon. Hudsons Bay Company, In presence of William Garrioch and James Asham.

Mowat, Charlotte: See William Smith and Charlotte Mowat

Mowat, Edward and Margaret: No. 407, Edward Mowat of Red River Settlement and Margaret Mowat of the same place were married at the Grand Rapids R.R.S. by banns with consent of Parents and Parties This Thirteenth Day of December, In the year one thousand eight hundred and Thirty eight, By me Wm. Cochran Asst. Chaplain to the H.H.B. Company. This marriage was solemnized between us Edward Mowat and Margaret (her X mark) Mowat, In the presence of Thomas Firth and George Ross.

Mowat, Edward and Mary: No. 323, Edward Mowat and Mary, his reputed wife were married at Red River Settlement with consent of parties, on the 17th December in the year 1836, by William Cochran 2nd Chaplain to the Hon. Hudson's Bay Company, Witnesses: James Corrigal and James Anderson.

Mowat, Jane: See Palm Saunders and Jane Mowat

Mowat, Jane: See Thomas Brown and Jane Mowat

Mowat, John and Frances Davis: No. 98, John Mowat, of Red River Settlement, and Frances Davis, of the same place, were married at the Grand Rapids by Banns with Consent of Parties this Fourth day of November in the year One thousand eight hundred and Forty One, by me Wm. Cochran Chaplain to the Hon. H. B. Company. This marriage was solemnized between us John Mowat and Frances Davis, In the presence of John Sutherland and Andrew Mowat.

Mowat, Margaret: See John Davidson and Margaret Mowat

Mowat, Margarret: See William McDonald and Margarret Mowat

Mowat, Mary: See Malcome Cummings and Mary Mowat

Mowat, Thomas and Mary Truthwaite: No. 138, Thomas Mowat, of The Red River Settlement, and Mary Truthwaite, of the same place, were married at the Grand Rapids, by Banns, with consent of Parents and parties, this sixth Day of February in the year One thousand eight hundred forty five By me Wm. Cochran Chaplain to the H. H. B. Company. This marriage was Solemnized between us: Thomas Mowat (by mark X), Mary Truthwaite, In the presence of Andrew Mowat and James Gunn.

Muir, John and Elizabeth Steward: No. 97, John Muir, of Red River Settlement, and Elizabeth Steward, of the same place, were married at the Grand Rapids by Banns with Consent of Parties this Sixteenth day of September in the year One thousand eight hundred and Forty One, by me Wm. Cochran Chaplain to the Hon. H. B. Company. This marriage was solemnized between us John Muir and Elizabeth Steward, In the presence of John Mowat and Andrew Mowat.

Munro, Ann: See Neil Campbell and Ann Munro

Munro, Robert and Christiana Fraser: No. 397, Robert Munro, bachelor, Red River Settlement, and Christiana Fraser, spinster, of the same place, were married at the Upper Church, by banns, with consent of Parents, this 24th day of December, in the year of our Lord, 1846, by me, J. Macallum, Solemnized between us Robert Munro and Christiana Fraser (her mark X), In the presence of Alexander Munro and John Fraser.

Murray, Donald and Jane Mary Heron: No. 367, Donald Murray of Red River Settlement and Jane Mary Heron of the same place were married by Banns with Consent of parties at Red River Settlement on the 17th day of August 1837, by David T. Jones, Chaplain to the Honble. Hudson's Bay Company, Witness: John Fraser.

Murray, Elizabeth: See William Stevenson and Elizabeth Murray

Murray, James and Elizabeth Holmes: No. 387, James Murray, of Red River Settlement and Elizabeth Holmes of the same place, were married by Banns with mutual consent on the 15th day of March in the year 1838, by David T. Jones Chaplain to the Honble Hudson's Bay Company, Witnesses: John Pritchard and Selkirk McKay.

Murwick, Jane See James Spence and Jane Murwick

Narquay, Harry and Mary Monkman: No. 321, Harry Narquay and Mary Monkman, were married at Red River Settlement by Banns with consent of parents and parties, on the 29th day of November in the year 1836, by David T. Jones, Chaplain to the Hon. Hudsons Bay Comp., Witnesses: James Monkman and John Lloyd.

Norn, William and Sarah Whitford: No. 200, William Norn, of the Parish of St.Andrews Red River Settlement, and Sarah Whitford, of the same place, were married in St.Andrews Church by banns and with consent of parties this Fifth day of December in the year one Thousand Eight hundred and fifty, By me, Robert James Missionary. This marriage was Solemnized between us William Norn and Sarah Whitford (by mark X), In the presence of Edward Kippling and Philip McDonald.

Norne, William and Catherine Birston: No. 185, William Norne, of the Orkney Glands [?], and Catherine Birston, of Red River Settlement, were married by banns with consent of parties at Red River Church on the 3rd day of December 1829, by David T. Jones Chaplain and Missionary, In the presence of James Bird and Latitia Bird.

Norquay, Henry and Anne Spence: No. 222, Henry Norquay and Anne Spence, both of this Red River Settlement, were married by Banns, with consent of Parties on the 4th Day of November 1831, by Wlliam

Hudson Bay Company Marriages 1820-1851

Cockran, Assistant Chaplain of the Honble. Hudson's Bay Company, Witness Present: John Park, James Spence.

Norquay, Isabella: See John Morwick and Isabella Norquay

Norquay, John and Isabella Truthwaite: No. 235, John Norquay and Isabella Truthwaite, both of Red River Settlement, were married by Banns with consent of Parties this 21st Day of February 1832, by William Cockran Assistant Chaplain to the Honble. Hudsons Bay Company, Witnesses Present: Alexander Kennedy Jr. and Jacob Truthwaite.

Norquay, John and Nancy Ward: No. 142, John Norquay, of The Red River Settlement, and Nancy Ward, of The same place, were married at the Rapids Church, by License, with consent of Parents, this ninth Day of October in the year One thousand eight hundred and Forty Five, By me, Wm. Cochran Chaplain to the H. H. B. Company. This marriage was solemnized between us: John Norquay, Nancy Ward (by mark X), In the presence of George Spence and Margarret Spence.

Norte, Martin and Catherine Treathly: No. 37, Martin Norte of the Red River Colony and Catherine Treathly of the same place were married at Fort Douglas By Banns, this Eleventh Day of November in the Year One thousand eight hundred and Twenty One, By me, John West, Chaplain, This Marriage was solemnized between us Martin Norte (x his mark) and Catherine Treathly (x her mark), In the Presence of Jno. Alley and A. MacDonald.

Nott, John and Mary: No. 125, John Nott, of Red River Settlement, and Mary Knott, of the same place, were married at the Grand Rapids by Banns with Consent of Parties this Sixth day of April in the year One thousand eight hundred and Forty Four, by me Wm. Cochran Chaplain to the Hon. H. B. Company. This marriage was solemnized between us John Nott (by mark X) and Mary Nott (by mark X), In the presence of Griffith Daniel and Jacob Daniel.

Oliver, Ann: See Magnus Brown and Ann Oliver

Paquet, Antoine and Augustine Marchant: No. 39, Antoine Paquet of the Red River Colony and Augustine Marchant of the same place were married at Fort Gilbralter By Banns, this First Day of January in the Year One thousand eight hundred and Twenty Two, By me, John West, Chaplain, This Marriage was solemnized between us Antoine Paquet and Augustine Marchant, In the Presence of Edw. Harrison and A. Macdonald.

Parenteau, Catherine: See Henry Hallett Junior and Catherine Parenteau

Park, Catherine: See John Cromertie and Catherine Park

Park, George and Julie de Boix: No. 140, George Park, of The Red River Settlement, and Julie de Boix, of the same place, were married at the Grand Rapids, by Banns, with consent of Parents and parties, this Twenty sixth Day of February in the year One thousand eight hundred forty five By me Wm. Cochran Chaplain to the H. H. B. Company. This marriage was Solemnized between us: George Park, Julie de Boix (by mark X), In the presence of George Spence and James Whiteway.

Park, Isabella: See George Harcus and Isabella Park

Hudson Bay Company Marriages 1820-1851

Park, Margaret: See John Irvine and Margaret Park

Parke, John and Margaret: No. 61, John Parke of the Red River Colony and Margaret, a Half Caste Woman of the Same place were married at the Red River Colony this Fifth day of June in the Year One thousand eight hundred twenty three, By me, John West, Chaplain. This Marriage was solemnized, John Parke and Margarette (x her Mark), In the Presence of Peter Corigle and George Spence (x his Mark).

Peebles, Ellen: See John Linklater and Ellen Peebles

Peebles, William and Catherine Arcus: No. 180, William Peebles, of the Red River Settlement and Catherine Arcus, of the same place, were married in the Rapids Church by Banns and with consent of Parties this First Day of March in the year One Thousand eight hundred and forty nine, By me, Robert James Missionary. This marriage was Solemnized between us William Peebles (his mark X) and Catherine Arcus (her mark X), In the presence of Andrew Mowat and Robert Peebles.

Peltier, Marie Juliane: See Simon Dazis and Marie Juliane Peltier

Picquette, Justine: See William Dickson and Justine Picquette

Planken, Rosina: See John Erhler and Rosina Plankin

Polander, Joseph and Christy Abertae: No. 43, Joseph Polander of the Red River Colony and Christy Aberlae of the same place were married at Fort Garry this Eighteenth Day of April the Year One thousand eight hundred and Twenty Two, By me, John West, Chaplain, This Marriage was solemnized between us Joseph Polander (x his mark) and Christy Aberlae (x her mark), In the Presence of Walther de Huser - Geo. Simpson.

Polson, Angus and Anne Henderson: No. 395, Angus Polson, bachelor, Red River Settlementt, and Anne Henderson, spinster, of the Red River Settlement, were married, at the Upper Church, by special license, with consent of parents, this Twenty Sixth day of November, on the year 1846, by me J. Macallum. This marriage was solemnized between us Angus Polson and Anne Henderson (her mark X), in the presence of Hugh Polson and Angus Henderson.

Polson, Anne: See John Matheson and Anne Polson

Polson, Donald and Anne Pritchard: No.__, Donald Polson, bachelor of Red River Settlement, and Anne Pritchard, spinster of the same place, were married at the Upper Church, by banns, with consent of parties, this Twenty second day of January in the year of our Lord One Thousand, Eight Hundred, and Forty Six, by me John Macdallum, Soliminzed between us: Donald Polson and Anne Pritchard, In the presence of: John Pritchard and Hugh Matheson.

Polson, Hugh and Janet Henderson: No. 368, Hugh Polson of Red River Settlement and Janet Henderson of the same place were married by Banns with Consent of parents and parties at Red River Settlement on the 26th day of October 1837, by David T. Jones, Chaplain to the Honble. Hudson's Bay Company, Witnesses: John Matheson and John Livingstone.

Hudson Bay Company Marriages 1820-1851

Polson, Jane: See John Sutherland and Jane Polson

Polson, John and Catharine Flett: No. 357, John Polson, of Red River Settlement, and Catharine Flett, of the same place, were married at the Upper Church by Banns with Consent of Parents and Parties this Seventh day of October in the year One thousand eight hundred and Forty One, by me Wm. Cochran Chaplain to the Hon. H. B. Company. This marriage was solemnized between us John Polson and Catharine Flett (by mark X), In the presence of Selkirk McKay and Angus McLeod.

Prince, George and Nancy Beardy: No. 370, George Prince of the Indian Settlement at Red River and Nancy Beardy of the same place, were married with mutual consent on the 22nd November in the year 1837, by William Cochran, 2nd Chaplain to the Honble Hudson's Bay Company, Witnesses: Joseph Cook and Peter Corrigal.

Prince, Jane: See George Taylor and Jane Prince

Prince, John and Margaret: No. 381, John Prince, of the Indian Settlement and Margaret Prince of the same place, were married by Banns with mutual consent on the 1st February 1838, by Wm. Cochran 2nd Chaplain to the Honble Hudson's Bay Company, Witnesses: Anne Cochran and Thomas Favel.

Pritchard, Anne: See Donald Polson and Anne Pritchard

Pritchard, Catherine: See John Matheson and Catherine Pritchard

Pritchard, John and Jannet Matheson: No. 423, John Pritchard, of Red River Settlement, and Jannet Matheson of the same place, were married at the the Elm's Cottage, by banns, with consent of parents and parties this Twelfth Day of December In the year One Thousand Eight Hundred and Thirty nine, By me William Cochran Asst. Chaplain to the H.H.B. Company. This marriage was Solemnized between us John Pritchard and Jannet Matheson, In the presence of John Pritchard and Angus Matheson.

Pritchard, Letitia: See Hugh Matheson and Letitia Pritchard

Pruden, Ann: See Duncan Campbell and Ann Pruden

Pruden, Charlotte: See John McLeod and Charlotte Pruden

Pruden, Charlotte: See Thomas Lions and Charlotte Pruden

Pruden, Cornelius and Isabella McKenzie: No. __, Cornelius Pruden, of the Red River Settlement, and Isabella McKenzie of the same place, were married at the Upper Church by Banns, with consent of Parents, on the 11th day of January in the year 1844, by me, Abraham Cowley, Missionary, Solemnized between us Cornelius Pruden and Isabella McKenzie, Witnesses: Jo. McCallum and Jo. Charles.

Pruden, James and Nancy Smith: No. 412, James Pruden of Red River Settlement and Nancy Smith of the same place were married at the middle Church R.R.S. by banns with the consent of Parents and Parties This fourteenth Day of March In the year one thousand eight hundred and thirty eight [nine?] By me Wm.

Hudson Bay Company Marriages 1820-1851

Cochran Asst Chaplain to the H.H.B. Company. This marriage was solemnized between us James (his X mark) Pruden and Nancy (her X mark) Smith, In the presence of William Norn and William Garrioch.

Pruden, John Peter and Anne Armstrong: No. 422, John Peter Pruden Esqr, Retired Chief Factor, Red River Settlement, and Miss Anne Armstrong, Governess to Mr. Mcalum, the same place, were married at the Upper Church, with consent of parties this fourth Day of December In the year One Thousand Eight Hundred and Thirty nine, By me William Cochran Asst. Chaplain to the H.H.B. Company. This marriage was Solemnized between us John Peter Pruden and Anne Armstrong, In the presence of Dun Finlayson and John Mcallum.

Pruden, Maria: See William Folster and Maria Pruden

Pruden, Maria: See William Hallet and Maria Pruden

Pruden, Peter and Josette Gothiver: Peter Pruden of Red River Settlement and Josette Gothiver of Red River Settlement, Married 7th May 1829 by the Rev. William Cockran, Assistant Chaplain to the H. B. Co., Witnesses: William Garrioch & William Pruden. (Denney) (List of HBC Marriages, Joanne J. Hughes, c1977)

Pruden, William and Nancy Henry: No. 123, William Pruden of Red River Colony, and Nancy Henry of same place, were married by Banns at Red River Settlement on the 4th day of September 1826 by David T. Jones Chaplain, In presence of William Robert Smith and Peter Pruden.

Quinche, Alfred and Marianne Monnier: No. 27, Alfred Quinche, Swiss, and Marianne Monnier, Swiss, were married at York Factory this 20th day of August 1821, by me John West, Chaplain, signed Alfred Quinche and Marianne Monnier, In the presence of Walton Hausar and Nicholas Garry.

Rayn, Michael and Nancy Budd: No. 149, Michel Rayn, A Native of Strasburg, France, and Nancy Budd, A Half Breed Woman of Red River, were married by Banns with mutual consent at Red River Settlement the 17th day of March in the year 1828, David T. Jones Chaplain and Missionary, Present at the Ceremony: William Garrioch and Henry Budd.

Rein, Nancy: See Horatio Nelson Calder and Nancy Rein

Rendesbergher, Elizabeth: See Antoine Brechler and Elizabeth Rendesbergher

Richards, James and Elizabeth Truthwaite: No. 139, James Richards, of The Red River Settlement, and Elizabeth Truthwaite, of the same place, were married at the Grand Rapids, by Banns, with consent of Parents and parties, this sixth Day of February in the year One thousand eight hundred forty five By me Wm. Cochran Chaplain to the H. H. B. Company. This marriage was Solemnized between us: James Richards (by mark X), Elizabeth Truthwaite, In the presence of Andrew Mowat and James Gunn.

Richards, Mary Ann: See Daniel Lilley and Mary Ann Richards

Richards, Mary: See James Corrigal and Mary Richards

Richards, Mary: See John Monkman and Mary Richards

Robelair, Catherine: See John Beads and Catherine Robelair

Robelair, Peter and Margarret: No. 144, Peter Robelair, of The Red River Settlement, and Margarret Robilair, of The same place, were married at the Grand Rapids, by Banns, with consent of Parties, this First Day of January in the year One thousand eight hundred and Forty Six, By me, Wm. Cochran Chaplain to the H. H. B. Company. This marriage was solemnized between us: Peter Robelair (by X mark), Margarret Robelair (by mark X), In the presence of John Foubster and George Davis.

Robertson, Alexander and Anne Stewart: No. 98, Alexander Robertson, H. B. Co.'s Service and Anne Stewart of Lesser Slave Lake were married April 28th [?] 1825 at York Facotry, with consent of Parents and parties by William Cochran, Assistant Chaplain to H. B. Co., In presence of George Simpson Esq. Governor of Rupert's Land and Alexander Stewart Esqure, Chief Factor of the Hudsons Bay Company, George Harbidge.

Robertson, Catherine: See John Forbister and Catherine Robertson

Robertson, Colin and Therese Chalifoux: **Colin Robertson married 25 Aug 1828 at Oxford House Therese Chalifoux. (List of HBC Marriages, Joanne J. Hughes, c1977)

Robertson, George and Nancy: No. 186, George Robertson of Red River Settlement and Nancy An Indian woman of the same place; were married at Red River Settlement by Banns with consent of parties on the 22nd day of September 1829 by William Cockran Assistant Anglican Missionary; In the presence of John James Smith and Jane Thomas.

Robertson, James and Margaret Stewart: **James Robertson married 25 Aug 1828 at Oxford House Margaret Stewart. (List of HBC Marriages, Joanne J. Hughes, c1977)

Robillard, Elizabeth: See Alexander McDonald and Elizabeth Robillard

Robinson, James and Margaret Atkinson: No. 268, John Robinson and Margaret Atkinson, were married by Banns at Red River Settlement 28th January 1834, by Wm. Cockran, Assistant Chaplain of the Hon. H. B. Company, Witnesses: Donald Gunn and Andrew McCorrister.

Robison, Andrew and Nancy Atkison: No. 220, Andrew Robison and Nancy Atkison, both of Red River Settlement, were married by Banns with Consent of Parties on the 1st day of September 1831, by William Cockran Assistant Chaplain to the Honble Hudson's Bay Company, Witnesses Present: Margaret Cummings and Hannah Cummings.

Robison, Ann: See Richard Smith and Ann Robison

Robison, George and Jane Johnstone: No. 436, George Robison, of Red River Settlement, and Jane Johnstone at the same place, were married at the Rapids, with consent of parties this This Nineteenth Day of August In the year 1840, By me William Cochran Asst. Chaplain to the H.H.B. Company. This marriage was solemnized between us George Robison (his mark X) and Jane Johnstone (her mark X), In the presence of Sarah Morwick and Ann Cochran.

Robison, Mary: See John Spence and Mary Robison

Rodway, Joseph and Betsy Stanley: No. 419, Joseph Rodway, Bachelor and pensioner, Red River Settlement, and Betsy Stanley, Spinster, of the same place, were married at the Upper Church, By Banns, with consent of Parties the first day of January in the year of our Lord 1849, by me, Wm. Cochran, Chaplain to the H. H. B. Co., Solemnized between us Joseph Rodway and Betsy Stanley, In the presence of Thomas Oakes and Catherine Oakes.

Rose, Betsy: See William Daniel and Betsy Rose

Rose, Isabella: See Hugh Livingstone and Isabella Rose

Rose, Margaret: See Daniel Esson and Margaret Rose

Ross, Alexander and Sally: **Alexander Ross and Sally married 24 Dec 1828. (Denney)

Ross, Clemence: See John Moore and Clemence Ross

Ross, Hugh and Sarah Short: No. 190, Hugh Ross, of White Horse Plains Settlement, and Sarah Short of the same place, were married at Red River Church by Banns on the 29th day of December 1829, by David T. Jones, Chaplain and Missionary, In the presence of William Garrioch and Alban Fidler.

Ross, Isabella: See William Gunn and Isabella Ross

Ross, Jean: See James Hunter and Jean Ross

Ross, Margaret: See Hugh Matheson and Margaret Ross

Ross, Mary: See George Flett and Mary Ross

Rowland, Gizzel: See James Birston and Gizzel Rowland

Rowland, Maria: See William Sletter and Maria Rowland

Rowland, Robert and Betsy Flett: No. 75, April 29th 1824, Robert Rowland and Betsy Flett, Witnesses: Wm. Gibson and John Park. Marriages celebrated at the Red River Colony from October 1823 to July 1824 by me, David T. Jones 2nd Chaplain.

Rowland, William and Betsy Ballenden: No. 395, William Rowland, a native of the Orkneys, and Betsy Ballenden, of Norway House, wre married by mutual consent at Norway House on the 21st day of August in the year one thousand eight hundred and thirty eight, by me David T. Jones Chaplain to the H. H. B. Company. This marriage was solemnized between us: William (his X mark) Rowland and Betsy (her X mark) Ballenden, In the presence of William Walls and David (his X mark) Johnson.

Rowland, William and Lusette Slater: No. 399, William Rowland, bachelor, Red River Settlement, and Susette Slater, spinster, of the same place, were married at the Upper Church, by banns, with consent of Parents, this 21st day of January, in the year of our Lord, 1847, by me, J. Macallum, Solemnized between us William Rowland and Susette Slater (her mark X), In the presence of James Slater and Peter Fidler.

Sabiston, Alexander and Nancy: No. 430, Alexander Sebister, of Red River Settlement, and Nancy Sebister of the same place, were married at Grand Rapids, by banns, with consent of parties this Fourth of March In the year One Thousand Eight Hundred and Forty, By me William Cochran Asst. Chaplain to the H.H.B. Company. This marriage was Solemnized between us Alexander Sebister's (his X mark) and Nancy Sebister's (her X mark), In the presence of Peter Pruden and James McKay.

Sabiston, Elizabeth: See Thomas Swain and Elizabeth Sabiston

Sabiston, Sarah: See William Taylor and Sarah Sabiston

Sanders, Margaret: See James Spence and Margaret Sanders

Sanders, William and Flora Hope: .No. 425, William Sanders, of Red River Settlement, and Flora Hope of the same place, were married at the Grand Rapids, by banns, with consent of parents and parties this Twenty sixth Day of December In the year One Thousand Eight Hundred and Thirty nine, By me William Cochran Asst. Chaplain to the H.H.B. Company. This marriage was Solemnized between us William Sanders (his X mark) and Flora Hope (her X mark), In the presence of James Linklater and Donald Spence.

Sanderson, Betsy: See David Johnson and Betsy Sanderson

Sanderson, George and Nancy: No. 208, George Sanderson, a Native Indian Cumberland House District and Nancy his reputed wife of the same place were married at the Red River Church on the 25th day of Novmeber 1840 by David T. Jones Chaplain to the Honble Husdons Bay Company, Witnesses Present: Robert Sandison and John Auld.

Sanderson, Robert and Mary Bear: No. 29, Robert Sanderson and Mary Bear, of Red River Colony, were married by Banns with consent of parties on the 31st day of March 1836, by David T. Jones, Chaplain to the Hon. H. Bay Company, Witnesses: Wm. Tate and John Spense.

Sandison, David and Louisa Goboche: No. 83, David Sandison and Louisa Goboche were married at Red River Settlement by Banns on the nineteenth of October 1824 by me, David T. Jones, Asst. Chaplain, In presence of Samuel Cook, George Harbidge.

Sandison, George and Jane Henderson: No. 7, George Sandison and Jane Henderson, both of Red River, were married by Banns on the 10th day of December 1835, by David T. Jones, Chapl. to The Hon. H. B. Compy., Witnesses: Philip Kennedy and John Spense.

Sandison, George and Mary Whitford: No. 117, George Sandison of Red River Settlement, and Mary Whitford, of the same place, were married at the Grand Rapids by Banns with Consent of Parents and Parties this Twelfth day of December in the year One thousand eight hundred and Forty Three, by me Wm.

Cochran Chaplain to the Hon. H. B. Company. This marriage was solemnized between us George Sandison (by mark X) and Mary Whitford (by mark X), In the presence of Samuel Whitford and George Spence.

Sandison, Isabella: See John Inkster and Isabella Sandison

Sandison, James and Ann Whitford: No. 229, James Sandison, widower, and Anne Whitford, both of Red River Settlement, were married by Banns with consent of Parties this 9th Day of February 1832 by David T. Jones Chaplain to the Honble Hudson's Bay Company, Witnesses Present: [missing].

Sandison, James and Elizabeth Anderson: No. 409, James Sandison, of Red River Settlement and Elisabeth Anderson of the same place, were married at the Grand Rapids by Banns, with consent of Parents and Parties, this twenty seventh day of December in the year one thousand eight hundred and thirty eight, by me, Wm. Cochran, Asst. Chapn. to the H. H. Bay Company. This marriage was solemnized between us James Sandison and Elizabeth Anderson, In the presence of John Mowat and John Hope.

Sandison, James and Margaret Louis: No. 138. James Sandison, A Half Breed Settler of R. R. Colony And Margaret Louis, A Negro Half Breed, of the same place here married at Red River Protestant Church, by Banns with mutual consent on the 3rd of November 1827, by David T. Jones Chaplain to the Hon. Hudsons Bay Co, In the presence of Robert Sandison, James Voller.

Sandison, James and Mary Faval: No. 112, James Sandison of Red River Settlement, and Mary Favel, of the same place, were married at the Grand Rapids by Banns with Consent of Parties this Twenty Third day of November in the year One thousand eight hundred and Forty Three, by me Wm. Cochran Chaplain to the Hon. H. B. Company. This marriage was solemnized between us James Sandison (by mark X) and Mary Favel (by mark X), In the presence of Thomas Lambier and Peter Henderson.

Sandison, Jenny: See Peter Tate and Jenny Sandison

Sandison, John and Elizabeth Sutherland: No. 438, John Sandison, Fort Simpson, McKenzie River District, and Elizabeth Sutherland, of the same place, were married at Fort Simpson with consent of Parties this First day of September in the year 1838 By me M. McPherson Magistrate, Solemnized between us John Sandison and Elizabeth Sutherland, In the presence of William Mowat and William Wilson.

Sandison, John and Harriett Smith: No. 273, John Sandison, an Indian and Harriett Smith, were married by Banns, on the 1st April 1834, by D. T. Jones Chaplain to the Honble. H. B. Company, Witnesses: William Tate and George Gual [?].

Sandison, Margaret: See Francis Desharim and Margaret Sandison

Sandison, Robert and Jane McNab: No. __, Robert Sandison, Widower, of Red River Settlement, and Jane McNab, spinster, of the same place, were married in the Upper Church, by special license and with consent of parties, this first day of June, in the year of our Lord, one thousand eight hundred and Forty Eight, By me, Wm. Cochran. This marriage was Solemnized between us Robert Sandison and Jane McNab, In the presence of Dominique Pambrun and Anne McDermot.

Sandison, Robert and Jane McNab: No. 413, Robert Sandison, Widower, of Red River Settlement, and Jane McNab, spinster, of the same place, were married in the Upper Church, by special license and with consent of parties, this first day of June, in the year of our Lord, one thousand eight hundred and Forty Eight, By me, Wm. Cochran. This marriage was Solemnized between us Robert Sandison and Jane McNab, In the presence of Dominique Pambrun and Anne McDermot.

Sandison, Sarah: See Samuel Spence and Sarah Sandison

Sandison, Sophia: See John Cook and Sophia Sandison

Sandison, William and Jane Badger: No. 192, William Sandison of Red River Settlement and Jane Badger of the same place, were married by Banns at Red River Colony on the 7th day of January 1830, by David T. Jones Chaplain & Missionary, In the presence of William Fisk and Robert Sandison.

Sandison, William and Margaret Cook: No. 104, December 2, 1825, William Sandison, of Red River Settlement, and Magaret Cook, of the same place, were married at Red River Settlement by Banns with consent of the Parents and Parties, by David T. Jones, Chaplain to The Hon. Hudsons Bay Company, In presence of Charles Cook and William Garrioch Schoolmaster.

Saunders, Anne: See Charles Fidler and Anne Saunders

Saunders, David and Sarah Saunders: No. 6, David Saunders and Sarah Saunders, both of Red River Settlement, were married by Banns on the 7th day of December 1835, by Wm. Cockran 2nd Chapln. to The Hon. H. B. Compy., Witnesses: John Linklater and James Lyons.

Saunders, Elizabeth: See John Linklater and Elizabeth Saunders

Saunders, John and Harriet Favel: No. 187, John Saunders, of Red River Settlement, and Harriet Favel of the same place, were married by Banns with consent of parties at Red River Church on the 23rd day of December 1829, by William Cockran Asst. Chaplain and Missionary, In the presence of William Robert Smith and William Sanderson.

Saunders, Margaret: See John Macnab and Margaret Saundrs

Saunders, Palm and Jane Mowat: No. 168, Palm Saunders, of the Red River Settlement, and Jane Mowat, of the same place, were married in the Rapids Church, by Banns, and with consent of the parties, this Sixth Day of April in the Year One Thousand eight Hudnred and forty Eight By me Robert James Missiionary. This marriage was solemnized between us Palm Saunders and Jane Mowat, In the presence of George Taylor and James Clouston.

Saunderson, George and Lisset Lajoumoniere: No. 18, George Saunderson, of Red River Colony and Lisset Lajoumoniere of the same place were married at Fort Douglas this Thirtieth Day of March in the Year One thousand eight hundred and Twenty-One, By me John West Chaplain, This Marriage was solemnized between us Geo. Saunderson (x his mark) and Lisset Lajoumoniere (x her mark), In the Presence of Thomas Thomas and Joseph Bird.

Hudson Bay Company Marriages 1820-1851

Saunderson, James and Sally: No. 66, October 31st, 1823, James Saunderson and Sally an Indian Woman, Witnesses: Wm. Sinclair x mark, David Sanderson x mark. Marriages celebrated at the Red River Colony from October 1823 to July 1824 by me, David T. Jones 2nd Chaplain.

Saunderson, Robert and Sennasso Halfbreed Woman: No. 7, Robert Saunderson of the Red River Colony and Sennecasso a halfbreed Woman of the same place were married at Fort Douglas this Twenty ninth Day of November in the year One thousand eight hundred and Twenty, By me John West Chaplain, This Marriage was solemnized between us Robt Saunderson (x his mark) and Sennecasso (x her mark), In the Presence of Donald Macdonnille and Joseph Bird.

Saunderson, William and Mary Alder: No. 197, William Sanderson, of the Red River Settlement, and Mary Alder, of the same place, were married at Red River Settlement by Banns with consent of parties on the 12th day of March 1830, by William Cockran Asst. Chaplain, In the presence of William Robert Smith and Richard Stevens.

Saundison, Elizabeth: See Thomas Smith and Elizabeth Saundison

Sauteaux Indian Woman, Mary: See Robert Logan and Mary a Sauteaux Indian Woman

Sauteux Indian Woman, Mary: See James Anderson and Mary a Sauteux Indian Woman

Scarth, John and Nelly Cree Indian Woman: No. 47 [sic], John Scarth of the Red River Colony and Nelly, a Cree Indian Woman, The Reputed wife of the late James Saunderson of the same place were married at Fort Garry this Eighteenth Day of June in the Year One thousand eight hundred and Twenty Two, By me, John West, Chaplain, This Marriage was solemnized between us John Scarth (x his mark) and Nelly (x his mark), In the Presence of George Harbidge and William Pruden.

Schmidt, Bernard and Susannah Aberlae: No. 45, Bernard Schmidt of the Red River Colony and Susannah Aberlae of the same place were married at Fort Garry this Second Day of May the Year One thousand eight hundred and Twenty Two, By me, John West, Chaplain, This Marriage was solemnized between us Bernard Schmidt (x his mark) and Susanna Abertae (x her mark0, In the Presence of Walther de Huser and Wm. Todd.

Schmidt, Mathias and Marianne Schudecker: No. 46, Mathias Schmidt of the Red River Colony and Marianne Schudecker of the same place were married at Fort Garry this Tenth Day of June in the Year One thousand eight hundred and Twenty Two, By me, John West, Chaplain, This Marriage was solemnized between us Mathias Schmidt and Marianne Schudecker (x her mark), In the Presence of Walther de Huser and George Harbidge.

Schudecker, Marianne: See Mathias Schmidt and Marianne Schudecker

Sellwood, John William and Delilah Good: No. 428, John Wm. Sellwood, pensioner and Bachelor, Red River Settlement, and Delilah Good, widow, of the same place, were married, by Banns, at the Upper Church with consent of parties, this 3rd day of April 1849, By me, Wm. Cochran, Chaplain to the H. H. B. Co., Solemnized between us John Wm. Sellwood and Delilah Good, In the presence of Thomas Heber [?] and James Harrison.

Hudson Bay Company Marriages 1820-1851

Settee, George and Margaret: No. 257, George Settee, an Indian, and Margaret, were married by Banns at Red River Settlement the 12th April 1833, By The Revd. D. T. Jones Chaplain to the Honble. Hudson's Bay Company, Witnesses Present: Robert Sanderson and Andrew McChorister.

Settee, James and Sarah Cook: No. 290, James Settee of Red River Colony, and Sarah Cook of the same place, were married by Banns at Red River on the 7th day of January in the year 1835, by Wm. Cockran 2nd Chaplain to the Hon. Hudson's Bay Compy. Witnesses: John James Smith and Joseph Cook.

Setter, Andrew and Margaret a halfbreed Woman: No. 12, Andrew Setter, of Beaver Creek and Margaret a halfbreed Woman of the same place were married at Beaver Creek this Twenty-eighth Day of January in the Year One thousand eight hundred and Twenty-One, By me John West Chaplain, This Marriage was solemnized between us Andrew Setter and Margaret (x her mark), In the Presence of Alexr Robertson and George McRae.

Setter, Elizabeth: See Robert Millar and Elizabeth Setter

Setter, George and Isabella Kennedy: No. 14, George Setter and Isabella Kennedy, both of Red River Settlement, were married by Banns on the 30th day of December 1835, by David T. Jones, Chaplain to The Hon. H. B. Compy., Witnesses: Alexander Christie and Charles Bird.

Setter, George and Margaret Setter: No. 126, George Setter, of Nettley Creek Trading post, and Margaret Setter, of this Colony, were married by Banns at Red River Settlement on the 8th day of December 1826 by David T. Jones Chaplain, In presence of James Monkman and John Park.

Setter, Isabella: See Joseph Monkman and Isabella Setter

Setter, James and Jane Morwick: No. 324, James Setter and Jane Morwick were married at Red River Settlement with consent of prties, on the 22nd December in the year 1836, by William Cochran 2nd Chaplain to the Hon. Hudson's Bay Company, Witnesses: William Corrigal and James Sutherland.

Setter, John and Nancy McKenzie: No. 186, John Setter, of Red River Settlement, and Nancy NcKenzie, of the same place, were married in the Rapid's Church by Banns and with consent of Parties this Twelfth day of July in the year One Thousand eight Hundred and forty nine, by me, Robert James Missionary. This marriage was Solemnized between us John Setter and Nancy McKenzie, In the presence of Andrew Setter and John Bruce.

Setter, Nancy: See James McKenzie and Nancy Setter

Short, James and Betsy Cree Indian Woman: No. 16, James Short, of Beaver Creek and Betsy, a Cree Indian Woman of the same place were married at Beaver Creek this Twenty-ninth Day of January in the Year One thousand eight hundred and Twenty-One, By me John West Chaplain, This Marriage was solemnized between us Jas. Short (x his mark) and Betsy (x her mark), In the Presence of Alexr Robertson and Andrew Setter.

Short, Jane: See Joseph White and Jane Short

Short, Sarah: See Hugh Ross and Sarah Short

Short, Susannah: See Pierre Ledoux and Susannah Short

Short, Suzette: See Samuel Cook and Suzette Short

Simon, George and Catherine Bunsley: No. 32, George Simon of the Red River Colony and Catherine Bunsley of the same place were married at Fort Douglas, this Fourth Day of November in the Year One thousand eight hundred and Twenty One, By me, John West, Chaplain, This Marriage was solemnized between us George Simon and Catherine Bunsley, In the Presence of Walher de Huser and Paul Regenberge.

Sinclair, Catherine: See Joseph Cook and Catherine Sinclair

Sinclair, Donald and Ann Gibson: No. 88, Donald Sinclair and Ann Gibson were married at Red River Settlement by Banns on the seventeenth day of December 1824, by me, David T. Jones, Asst. Chaplain, In presence of George McKirk, Hugh Livingstone.

Sinclair, Francis and Maria: No. 26, The marriage between Francis Sinclair and Maria, both Cree Indians, was solemnized at the Church Indian Settlement this 15th day of December 1844. (All the signatures not copied)

Sinclair, George and Ann Johnston: No. 429, George Sinclair, of Red River Settlement, and Ann Johnston of the same place, were married at Grand Rapids, by banns, with consent of parties this Fourth of March In the year One Thousand Eight Hundred and Forty, By me William Cochran Asst. Chaplain to the H.H.B. Company. This marriage was Solemnized between us George Sinclair (his X mark) and Ann Johnston (her X mark), In the presence of Peter Pruden and James McKay.

Sinclair, James and Elizabeth Bird: No. 184, James Sinclair, of Red River Settlement, and Elizabeth Bird of the same place, married by Banns with consent of parties at Red River Church on 3 Dec 1829, David T. Jones Chaplain and Missionary, In the presence of James Bird and Latitia Bird.

Sinclair, James and Mary Campbell: No. __, James Sinclair, Widower, of Red River Settlement, and Mary Campbell, spinster, of the same place, were married in the Upper Church, by special license and with consent of parties, this twentieth day of April, in the year of our Lord, one thousand eight hundred and Forty Eight, By me, Wm. Cochran. This marriage was Solemnized between us James Sinclair and Mary Campbell, In the presence of Alexr. Christie, John Bunn and John McLoughlin.

Sinclair, James and Mary Campbell: No. 412, James Sinclair, Widower, of Red River Settlement, and Mary Campbell, spinster, of the same place, were married at Mr. Sinclair's Establishment by special license and with consent of parties, this twentieth day of April, in the year of our Lord, one thousand eight hundred and Forty Eight, By me, Wm. Cochran. This marriage was Solemnized between us James Sinclair and Mary Campbell, In the presence of Alexr. Christie, John Bunn and John McLoughlin.

Sinclair, Margaret: See William Gibboo and Margaret Sinclair

Hudson Bay Company Marriages 1820-1851

Sinclair, Mary: See John Inkster and Mary Sinclair

Sinclair, Phoebe: See Thomas Bunn and Phoebe Sinclair

Sinclair, Thomass and Hannah Cummings: No. 230, Thomas Snclair and Hannah Cummings, both of Red River Settlement, were married by Banns with consent of Parties on the 9th Day of February 1832, by William Cockran Assistant Chaplain to the Honble. Hudson's Bay Company, Witnesses Present: Alexander Kennedy Junr. and ...

Sinclair, William and Elizabeth Anderson: No. 112, January 31, 1826, William Sinclair, of Red River, and Elizabeth Anderson, of the same place, were married at Red River Settlement by Banns with consent of the parties by David T. Jones Chaplain to The Hon. Husdon's Bay Company, In the presence of High Gibson and James Anderson settlers.

Sinclair, Wm. And Mary McKay: No. 63, Wm. Sinclair of Norway House, and Mary McKay of the same place were married at Norway House this Twenty first day of June on the year One Thousand Eight Hundred and Twenty Three, by me, John West, Chaplain. This Marriage was Solemnized between us Wm Sinclair and Mary McKay (x her mark), In the presence of D. McKenzie, Ronnie McKenzie, Peter [?].

Slater, Isabella: See Henry Brown and Isabella Slater

Slater, John and Elizabeth Dennett: No. 119, July 11, 1826, John Slater, of Orkney, North Britain, and Elizabeth Dennett, of Red River Settlement, were married by Banns with consent of parties at Red River Settlement by David T. Jones, Chaplain to The Hon. Husdon's Bay Company, In presence of Joseph Bois and John Levingstone.

Slater, Lusette: See William Rowland and Lusette Slater

Sletter, Charlotte: See Clement Fidler and Charlotte Sletter

Sletter, James and Mary: No. 145, James Sletter, of Kirkwall in the Isle of Pomona, Orkney, and Mary, An Indian Woman from James's Bay, were married at Red River Settlement by Banns with mutual consent on the 27th day of December 1827, David T. Jones Chaplain and Missionary, Present at the ceremony: William Taylor and Andrew Setter.

Sletter, William and Maria Rowland: No. 446, William Sletter, of Red River Settlement, and Maria Rowland, of the same place, were married at the Rapids by banns, with consent of Parents and Parties this Twenty First day of January in the year 1841 By me William Cochran Asst. Chaplain to the H.H.B. Company. Solemnized between us William Sletter and Maria Rowland, In the presence of John Sutherland and John Mowat.

Smith, Alexander and Nancy Bear: No. 248, Alexander Smith, an Indian, and Nancy Bear, his reputed wife, were married by Banns at Red River Settlement, 20th November 1832, by Rev. D. T. Jones Chaplain to the Honble. Hudsons Bay Company, Witnesses Present: Robert Sandison and Jacob Bear.

Hudson Bay Company Marriages 1820-1851

Smith, Elizabeth: See David Bear and Elizabeth Smith

Smith, Harriett: See John Sandison and Harriett Smith

Smith, Harriot: See James Anderson and Harriot Smith

Smith, Jacob and Jane: No. 246, Jacob Smith and Jane, an Indian woman,, were married by Banns at Red River Settlement 25th October 1832, by Rev. D. T. Jones, Chaplain to the Honble. Hudson Bay Company, Witnesses Present: Robert Sandison and Thomas Thomas.

Smith, Jane: See John Ashim and Jane Smith

Smith, John and Mary Taylor: No. 162, John Smith, of the Red River Settlementk and Mary Taylor, of the same place, were married in the Rapids Church, by Banns, and with consent of parties, This Eight day of April in the year one Thousand eight hundred and Forty Seven by me Robert James Missionary. This marriage was Solemnized between us: John Smith and Mary Taylor, In the presence of John James Smith and Alexander Thomas.

Smith, John James and Mary: No. 95, John James Smith and Mary an Indian Woman, were married at Red River Settlement on the 12th day of July 1825, by me, David T. Jones, Assistant Chaplain, In presence of William Garrioch and Joseph Cook.

Smith, John James and Nancy Favel: No. 297, John James Smith, of Red River Colony, and Nancy Favel of the same place, were married at Red River by Banns on the 29th day of April in the year 1835, by Wm. Cockran 2nd Chaplain to Honorable Hudson's Bay Company, Witnesses: Joseph Cook and Catherine Cook.

Smith, John Lee Lewis and Elizabeth Moor: No. 121, John Lee Lewis Smith, of Red River Settlement, and Elizabeth Moor, of the same place, were married at the Grand Rapids by Banns with Consent of Parents and Parties this Twenty Eight day of December in the year One thousand eight hundred and Forty Three, by me Wm. Cochran Chaplain to the Hon. H. B. Company. This marriage was solemnized between us John Lee Lewis Smith and Elizabeth Moor (by mark X), In the presence of James Gunn and John McDonald.

Smith, Nancy: See James Pruden and Nancy Smith

Smith, Peter and Susan Peyronette: No. 275, Peter Smith, a native Indian and Susan Peyronette, an Indian Woman, were married by Banns on the 29th May 1834, by Wm. Cockran, Assistant Chaplain to the Honble. H. B. Company, Witnesses: Robert Sandison.

Smith, Richard and Ann Robison: No. 420, Richard Smith of Red River Settlement, and Ann Robison of the same place, were married at the Grand Rapids, by banns, with consent of parties this seventh Day of November In the year One Thousand Eight Hundred and Thirty nine, By me William Cochran Asst. Chaplain to the H.H.B. Company. This marriage was Solemnized between us Richard Smith and Ann Robison, In the presence of John James Smith and Richard Stevens.

Smith, Richard and Catherine Thomas: No. 135, Richard Smith, of The Red River Settlement, and Catherine Thomas, of the same place, were married at the Grand Rapids, by Banns, with consent of Parents and parties this Seventh Day of January in the year One thousand eight hundred forty five By me Wm. Cochran Chaplain to the H. H. B. Company. This marriage was Solemnized between us: Richard Smith (by mark X), Catherine Thomas (by mark X), In the presence of John James Smith and Thomas Truthwaite.

Smith, Robert and Charlotte Smith: No. 380, Robert Smith, of the Indian Settlement and Charlotte Smith of the same place, were married by Banns with mutual consent on the 31st Jan, 1838, by Wm. Cochran 2nd Chaplain to the Honble Hudson's Bay Company, Witnesses: John James Smith and Nancy Smith.

Smith, Robert and Nancy Spence: No. 27, The marriage between Robert Smith and Nancy Spence, both Cree Indians, was solemnized at the Church Indian Settlement this 25th day of December 1844. (All the signatures not copied)

Smith, Thomas and Elizabeth Saundison: No. 396, Thomas Smith, bachelor, Red River Settlement, and Elizabeth Saundison, spinster, of the same place, were married at the Upper Church, by banns, with consent of Parents, this Seventeenth day of December, in the year of our Lord, 1846, by me, J. Macallum, Solemnized between us Thomas Smith (his mark X) and Elizabeth Saundison, In the presence of John Sutherland and Alexr. Matheson.

Smith, William and Charlotte Mowat: No. 194, William Smith, of the parish of St.Andrews Red River Settlement, and Charlotte Mowat, of the same place, were married in St.Andrew's Church by Banns and with consent of parties this Twelfth day of February in the year one Thousand Eight hundred and fifty, By me, Robert James Missionary. This marriage was Solemnized between us William Smith (by mark X) and Charlotte Mowat (by mark X), In the presence of Robert Mowat and John Gunn.

Smith, William and Patience Howell: No. 418, William Smith, Bachelor, Red River Settlement, and Patience Howell, spinster, of the same place, were married at the Upper Church, by Banns, with consent of parties, this sixteenth day of October, in the year of our Lord, One Thousand Eight Hundred and Forty Eight, By me, W. Cochran, Chaplain to the H. B. Co., Solemnized between us W. Smith and Patience Howell, In the presence of James Rickards and H. Rickards.

Smythe, William Robert and Mary Anne Swaine: No. 93, William Robert Smythe and Mary Anne Swaine, were married at the Red River Settlement, by Banns on the 15th day of July 1825 by me, David T. Jones Assistant Chaplain, In presence of Wm. Garrioch and Joseph Cook.

Southward Indian Woman, Mary: See Thomas Halcrow and Mary Southward Indian Woman

Spence, Andrew and Margaret a Cree Indian Woman: No. 11, Andrew Spence, of Brandon House and Margaret a Cree Indian Woman of the same place were married at Brandon House this Twenty third Day of January in the Year One thousand eight hundred and Twenty-One, By me John West Chaplain, This Marriage was solemnized between us Andr. Spence (x his mark) and Margaret (her mark), In the Presence of John Richards McKay and George McRae.

Spence, Andrew and Susette L'unay: No. 134, Andrew Spence, A Half Breed of Red River Settlement, and Susette L'Eunay, A Canadian Half Breed of the Saskatchewan, were married by Banns with consent of parties at Red River Colony on the 30th day of October 1827, by David T. Jones Chaplain to the H. H. B. Company, Present at the ceremony James Spence and Robert Sandison.

Hudson Bay Company Marriages 1820-1851

Spence, Anne: See Henry Norquay and Anne Spence

Spence, Archibald Stewart and Margaret: No. 148, Archibald Stewart Spence, of the Orkney Islands, and Margaret an Indian Woman from Severs Factory, were married at Red River Settlement by Banns with mutual consent on the 23rd day of February 1828, by David T. Jones Chaplain and Missionary, Witnesses present at the Ceremony: Joseph Spence and James Spence.

Spence, Catherine: No. 114, George Kepling of Red River Settlement, and Catherine Spence, of the same place, were married at the Grand Rapids by Banns with Consent of Parents and Parties this Thirteenth day of November in the year One thousand eight hundred and Forty Three, by me Wm. Cochran Chaplain to the Hon. H. B. Company. This marriage was solemnized between us George Kepling (by mark X) and Catherine Spence (by mark X), In the presence of Charles Anderson and Nicholas Spence.

Spence, Catherine: See Charles Begg and Catherine Spence

Spence, Catherine: See George Kepling and Catherine Spence

Spence, Charlotte: See George Groat and Charlotte Spence

Spence, Chloe: See James Whiteway and Chloe Spence

Spence, Christy: See Peter Whitford and Christy Spence

Spence, David and Catherine Hallet: No. __, David Spence, Bachelor, of the Red River Settlement, and Catherine Hallett, Spinster, of the same place, were married at the Upper Church, with consent of Parents, on the 15th day of February in the year 1844, By me, Abraham Cowley, Missionary, Solemnized between us David Spence and Catherine Hallet, Witnesses: James Spence and John ...

Spence, Donald and Nancy Arkus: No. 99, Donald Spence, of Red River Settlement, and Nancy Arkus, of the same place, were married at the Grand Rapids by Banns with Consent of Parties this Eighteenth day of September in the year One thousand eight hundred and Forty One, by me Wm. Cochran Chaplain to the Hon. H. B. Company. This marriage was solemnized between us Donald Spence (by mark X) and Nancy Arkus (by mark X), In the presence of Collin Bruce and Nicholas Spence.

Spence, Eleanor: See Jeremiah Cook and Eleanor Spence

Spence, Elizabeth: See William Leith and Elizabeth Spence

Spence, George and Catherine: No. 150, George Spence of Berens Island Orkneys and Catherine Sarcee Indian Woman, were married by Banns [..] at the Rapids of the Red River on the 17th day of May 1828, by David T. Jones Chaplain & Missionary, Witnesses: Wm ... and John Park.

Spence, George and Nancy Ward: No. 21, George Spence, of Red River Settlement and Nancy Ward of the same place were married at Fort Douglas this Sixth Day of May in the Year One thousand eight hundred and Twenty-One, By me John West Chaplain, This Marriage was solemnized between us George Spence (x his mark) and Nancy Ward (x her mark), In the Presence of George Harbidge and Peter Corricle.

Spence, Isabel: John Forbes and Isabel Spence

Spence, James and Jane Murwick: No. 47, James Spence of the Red River Colony and Jane Murwick of the same place were married at Fort Garry this Seventeenth Day of June in the Year One thousand eight hundred and Twenty Two, By me, John West, Chaplain, This Marriage was solemnized between us James Spence and Jane Murwick (x her mark), In the Presence of George Harbidge and Peter Pruden.

Spence, James and Margaret Lewis: No. 158, James Spence, of the Red River Settlement, and Margaret Lewis, of the Same place, were married in the Rapids Church, by Banns, with consent of Parties, This Seventeenth Day of December the year One Thousand Eight Hundred and Forty Six By me Robert James Missionary. This marriage was Solemnized between us: James Spence (his X mark) and Margaret Lewis (her X mark X), In the presence of John Slatter and Nicholas Spence

Spence, James and Margaret Sanders: No. 391, James Spence, of the Red River Settlement and Margaret Sanders of the same place, were married by Banns with consent of parents and parties on the Eighteenth day of July in the year one thousand eight hundred and thirty eight by William Cochran Asst. Chaplain to the Honble Hudson's Bay Company, Witnesses: Ann Cochran and Charlotte Bird.

Spence, James and Mary: No. 191, James Spence, of Red River Settlement and Mary a Native woman of the same place, were married by Banns with consent of parties at Red River, on the 5th day of January 1830, by David T. Jones Chaplain & Missionary, In the presence of Joseph Cook and Thomas Halcrow.

Spence, James and Nancy Whiteway: No. 414, James Spence of Red River Settlement and Nancy Whiteway of the same place were married at the Grand Rapids R.R.S. by banns with the consent of Parents and Parties This twenty second Day of April In the year one thousand eight hundred and thirty nine By me Wm. Cochran Asst Chaplain to the H.H.B. Company. This marriage was solemnized between us James (his X mark) Spence and Nancy (her X mark) Whiteway, In the presence of Joseph Monkman and James Whiteway.

Spence, Jane: See Antoine Hallet and Jane Spence

Spence, Jannet: See Henry Howes and Jannet Spence

Spence, John and Anne Spence: No. 386, John Spence, of the Indian Settlement and Anne Spence of the same place, were married by Banns with consent of parties on the 3rd day of April in the year 1838, by William Cochran 2nd Chaplain to the Honble Hudson's Bay Company, Witnesses: Ann Cochran and William King.

Spence, John and Charlotte Spence: No. 377, John Spence, of the Indian Settlement at the Red River, and Charlotte Spence, of the same place, were married by Banns with consent of parties on the 2nd day of January in the year One Thousand Eight hundred and Thirty Eight, by William Cochran, 2nd Chaplain to the Honble Hudson's Bay Company, Witnesses: John Spence and Thomas Cochran.

Spence, John and Charlotte Whitford: No. 172, John Spence, of the Red River Settlement, and Charlotte Whitford, of the Indian Settlement, were married in the Rapids Church, by Banns and with consent of Parties, this Eleventh day of September in the year One Thousand Eight hundred and forty Eight, By me, Robert James Missionary. This marriage was solemnized between us, John Spence (his mark X) and Charlotte Whitford (her mark X), In the presence of us Andrew Spence (his mark X) and Peter Whitford (his mark X).

Spence, John and Isabella Isham: No. 267, John Spence and Isabella Ishaml, were married by Banns at Red River Settlement 23rd January 1834, by Wm. Cockran, Assistant Chaplain of the Hon. H. B. Company, Present: John Slater and Peter Erasmus.

Spence, John and Jane Favel: No. 261, John Spence and Jane Favel, were married by Banns at Red River Settlement 17th September 1833 by Wm. Cockran, Assistant Chaplain of the Hon. Hudson's Bay Company, Witnesses Present: Griffith Daniel and Peter Garrioch.

Spence, John and Jane Taite: No. 4, John Spence of the Red River Colony and Jane Taite of the same place were married at Fort Douglas, by Banns with Consent of Parents this Twenty-seventh Day of November in the Year One thousand eight hundred and Twenty, By me John West Chaplain, This Marriage was solemnized between us John Spence (x his mark) and Jane Taite (x her mark), In the Presence of Wm. Laidlaw and Joseph Bird.

Spence, John and Margaret Dennet: No. 226, John Spence and Margaret Dennet both of Red River Settlement were married by Banns with Consent of Parties this 8th Day of December 1831, by William Cochran Assist. Chaplain to the Honble Hudson's Bay Company. Witnesses: Thomas Halcrow, Andrew Kennedy Junr.

Spence, John and Mary Robison: No. 394, John Spence, a native of Orkney, North Britain and Mary Robison, of Berens River House, were married by mutual consent at Berens River House, on the seventeenth of August one thousand eight hunddred and thirty eight, By me David T. Jones Chaplain to the H. H. B. Company. This marriage was solemnized between us John (his X mark) Spence and Mary (her X mark) Robison, In the presence of John Lloyd and Mary Ross.

Spence, John Clarke and Annabella McKenzie: No. 242, John Clarke Spence and Annabella McKenzie, were married by Banns at Red River Settlement the 11th September 1832, by David T. Jones Chaplain to the Honble. Hudsons Bay Company, Witnesses Present: Robert Clouston and Wm. Robt. Smith.

Spence, Joseph and Sally Jefferson: No. 64, Joseph Spence, of York Factory, and Sally Jefferson, of the same place, were married at York Factory, this Sixth day of July in the year One Thousand Eight Hundred and Twenty Three, by me, John West, Chaplain. This marriage was solemnized, Joseph Spence and Sally Jefferson (x her mark), In the Presence of Dond McKenzie and Jn [?] Robertson and Harry Gay.

Spence, Letitia: See Thomas Hay and Letitia Spence

Spence, Magnus and Sally Favel: No. 276, Magnus Spence, of the Red River Settlement, and Sally Favel, of the same place, were married by Banns at Red River Settlement 11th August 1834, by D. T. Jones Chaplain to the Honble. Hudson's Bay Company, Witnesses: Donald Spence and Geo. Setter.

Hudson Bay Company Marriages 1820-1851

Spence, Margaret: See Charles Cook and Margaret Spence

Spence, Margaret: See Francis Desmarais and Margaret Spence

Spence, Maria: See Simon Whitford and Maria Spence

Spence, Mary: See James Whitford and Mary Spence

Spence, Nancy: See Robert Smith and Nancy Spence

Spence, Nicholas and Sophia Thomas: No. 204, Nicholas Spence, of the Parish of the St.Andrews, Red River Settlement, and Sophia Thomas, of the same place, were married in St.Andrews Church by banns and with consent of parties this Twenty second day of May in the year one Thousand Eight hundred and fifty one, By me, Robert James Missionary. This marriage was Solemnized between us Nicholas Spence and Sophia Thomas (X), In the presence of William Linklater and Madalane Corrigal.

Spence, Peter and Terresia Bruce: No. 421, Peter Spence of Red River Settlement, and Terresia Bruce of the same place, were married at the Grand Rapids, by banns, with consent of parties this fifth Day of December In the year One Thousand Eight Hundred and Thirty nine, By me William Cochran Asst. Chaplain to the H.H.B. Company. This marriage was Solemnized between us Peter Spence (by mark X) and Terresia Bruce (by mark X), In the presence of Joseph Halcro and Mary Buxton.

Spence, Samuel and Jane Whitford: No. 389, Samuel Spence, of the Indian Settlement on Red River and Jane Whitford of the Red River Settlement, were married by Banns with consent of parties on the 17th day of May in the year 1838, by William Cochran 2nd Chaplain to the Honble Hudson's Bay Company, Witnesses: Anne Cochran and Thomas Lambere.

Spence, Samuel and Sarah Sandison: No. 178, Samuel Spence, of the Red River Settlement and Sarah Sandison of the same place, were married in the Rapids Church by Banns and with consent of Parties this Twenty Eight Day of February in the year One Thousand eight hundred and forty nine, By me, Robert James Missionary. This marriage was Solemnized between us Samuel Spence (his mark X) and Sarah Sandison (her mark X), In the presence of Henry Anderson (his mark X) and James Sinclair.

Spence, Sophia: See John Flett and Sophia Spence

Spence, William and Lorain Grachu: No. 272, William Spence and Lorain Grachu, were married by Banns at Red River Settlement 6th March 1834, by Wm. Cockran, Assistant Chaplain to the Honble. H. B. Company, Witnesses: Colin Leslie and William Cockran.

Spense, Catherine: See Peter De Boish and Catherine Spence

Spense, Isabella: See James Louis and Isabella Spense

Stanley, Betsy: See Joseph Rodway and Betsy Stanley

Hudson Bay Company Marriages 1820-1851

Stead, Ann: See George Atkinson and Ann Stead

Stead, Sarah: See James Corrigal and Sarah Stead

Stephenson, Samuel and Mary: No. 343, Samuel Stephenson and Mary, his reputed wife were married at Red River Settlement on the 8th day of March 1837, by William Cochran, 2nd Chaplain to the Honble. Hudson's Bay Company, Witnesses: Peter Corrigal and Joseph Cook.

Stevens, Isabella: See James Young and Isabella Stevens

Stevens, Richard and Mary: No. 135, Richard Stevens, Native of England, and Mary, a Native Woman from the Coast of Hudson's Bay, were married by Banns with consent by parties at Red River Colony on the 27th day of November 1827 by D. T. Jones Chaplain of the Hudson's Bay Company, Present at the ceremony: Donald Gunn and John McDonald.

Stevens, Thurza: See Charles Fox and Thurza Stevens

Stevenson, Jane: See John Thomas and Jane Stevenson

Stevenson, John and Betsy: No. 336, John Stevenson and Betsy, his reputed wife, were married at Red River Settlement by Banns on the 8th day of February 1837, by William Cochran, 2nd Chaplain to the Honble. Hudson's Bay Company, Witnesses: Joseph Cook and John James Smith.

Stevenson, John Thomas and Betsy Johnstone: No. 378, John Thomas Stevenson, of the Indian Settlement at Red River, and Betsy Johnstone, of the same place, were married by Banns with consent of parties on the 2nd day of January 1838, by William Cochran, 2nd Chaplain to the Honble Hudson's Bay Company, Witnesses: Joseph Cook and Peter Corrigal.

Stevenson, Mary: See Alexander Thomas and Mary Stevenson

Stevenson, William and Elizabeth Murray: No. __, William Stevenson, a native of Orkney, now of Red River Settlement, and Elizabeth Murray, widow, of the same place, were married at the Upper Church, with mutual consent of Parties, on the 20th day of March in the year 1844, By me, Abraham Cowley, Missionary, Solemnized between us William Stevenson and Elizabeth Murray, Witnesses: Donald Murray and John Auld.

Stevenson, William and Mary: No. 337, William Stevenson and Mary, his reputed wife, were married at Red River Settlement by Banns with mutual consent on the 8th day of February 1837, by William Cochran, 2nd Chaplain to the Honble. Hudson's Bay Company, Witnesses: Joseph Cook and John James Smith.

Steward, Elizabeth: See John Muir and Elizabeth Steward

Stewart, Anne: See Alexander Robertson and Anne Stewart

Stewart, Harriet: See Thomas Thomas and Harriet Stewart

Hudson Bay Company Marriages 1820-1851

Stewart, Margaret: See James Robertson and Margaret Stewart

Stodgell, Charles and Margaret Burke: No. 424, Charles Stodgell, Bachelor and Pensioner, Red River Settlement, and Margaret Burke, Spinster, of the same place, were married at the Upper Church, by license, with consent of Parents and Parties, this 16th day of Feb in the year1849, by me, Wm. Cochran, Chaplain to the H. H. B. Co., Solemnized between us C. Stodgell and Margaret Burke, In the presence of James Rickards and Nancy Burke.

Stranger, Robert and Nancy Bear: No. 240, Robert Stranger and Nancy Bear were married by Banns at Red River Settlement the 22nd Day of August 1832, by David T. Jones Chaplain to the Honble. Hudsons Bay Company, Witnesses Present: Robert Sanderson and Isabella Sanderson.

Stranger, Thomas and Elizabeth: No. 341, Thomas Stranger and Elizabeth, his reputed wife were married at Red River Settlement by Banns on the 8th day of March 1837, by William Cochran, 2nd Chaplain to the Honble. Hudson's Bay Company, Witnesses: Peter Corrigal and Joseph Cook.

Sutherland Louisa: See Thomas Bremner and Louisa Sutherland

Sutherland, Alexander and Christiana McBeath: No. 328, Alexander Sutherland and Christiana McBeath, were married by Banns with consent of parties on the 29th December1836, by William Cochran 2nd Chaplain to the Hon. Hudson's Bay Company, Witnesses: George Sutherland and Donald Murray.

Sutherland, Catherine: George McBeath and Catherine Sutherland

Sutherland, Catherine: See Arthur Campbell and Catherine Sutherland

Sutherland, Donald and Anne Livingstone: No. 283, Donald Sutherland, of the Red River Settlement, and Anne Livingstone, of the same place, were married by Banns on the 27th day of November in the year 1834, by D. T. Jones Chaplain to the Honble. Hudson's Bay Company, In presence: Morrison McBeath and Neil Livingstone.

Sutherland, Donald and Anne Matheson: No. 232, Donald Sutherland and Anne Matheson both of Red River Settlement were married by Banns with consent of Parties this 15th Day of February 1832, by D. T. Jones, Chaplain to the Honble. Hudsons Bay Company, Witnesses Present: James Matheson and Alexander Sutherland.

Sutherland, Ebenezer and Sarah Bunn: No. 182, Ebenezer Sutherland, of Red River Settlement, and Sarah Bunn, of the same place, were married by Banns with consent of Parents and Parties at Red River Church on the 19th day of November 1829, by David T. Jones Chaplain and Missionary, In presence of Thomas Bunn and John McIntyre.

Sutherland, Elizabeth: See James Inkster and Elizabeth Sutherland

Sutherland, Ellen: See George Macrae and Ellen Sutherland

Hudson Bay Company Marriages 1820-1851

Sutherland, George and Anne Sutherland: No. 339, George Sutherland and Anne Sutherland were married at Red River Settlement by Banns with consent of parties on the 28th day of February 1837, by William Cochran, 2nd Chaplain to the Honble. Hudson's Bay Company, Witnesses: Simon Thomas and John Cochran.

Sutherland, George and Henrietta Gunn: No. 369, George Sutherland of Red River Settlement and Henrietta Gunn of the same place were married by Banns with Consent of parents parties at Red River Settlement on the 9th day of November 1837, by David T. Jones, Chaplain to the Honble. Hudson's Bay Company, Witnesses: John Fraser and Hugh Matheson.

Sutherland, James and Betsy Calder: No. 178, James Sutherland of Red River Settlement and Betsey Calder of the same place, were married by Banns with mutual consent of parties on the 12th day of May 1829 by William Cockran, Assistant Chaplain, In the presence of William Garrioch and Henry Budd.

Sutherland, James and Jane Flett: No. 151, James Sutherland, ... of the Hon. Hudson's Bay Company and Jane Floett A Half Breed Woman, were married ... by mutual consent on the 20th day of May 1828, by David T. Jones Chaplain and Missionary, Present at the ceremony: Thos. Thomas and Thomas Bunn.

Sutherland, James and Maria Bird: No. 400, James Sutherland of the Red River Settlement and Maria Bird of the same place were married at the Middle Church RRS by banns with consent of Parents and Parties This first day of November, In the year one thousand eight hundred and thirty eight, By me Wm. Cochran Asst. Chaplain to the H. H. B. Company. This marriage was solemnized between us James Sutherland and Maria (her X mark) Bird, In the presence of W. Rob. Smith and James Tate.

Sutherland, Jeremiah and Margaret Sutherland: No. 70, December 23rd, 1823, Jeremiah Sutherland and Margaret Sutherland, Witnesses: Alexander McLeod, George Harbidge. Marriages celebrated at the Red River Colony from October 1823 to July 1824 by me, David T. Jones 2nd Chaplain.

Sutherland, John and Catherine Matheson: **John Sutherland, married 22 Jan 1829, Catherine Matheson. (Denney)

Sutherland, John and Jane Polson: No. 335, John Sutherland and Jane Polson were married at Red River Settlement by Banns on the 7th day of February 1837, by David T. Jones, Chaplain to the Honble. Hudson's Bay Company, Witnesses: John Matheson, Donald Murray, John Fraser.

Sutherland, John and Margaret Tate: No. 403, John Sutherland, bachelor, Red River Settlement, and Margaret Tate, spinster, of the same place, were married at the Upper Church, by banns, with consent of parents, this first day of April, in the year of our Lord, 1847, by me, John Macallum, Solemnized between us John Sutherland and Margaret Tate (her mark X), In the presence of William Tate and Alexr. Matheson.
Sutherland, Letitia: See James Inkster and Letitia Sutherland

Sutherland, Margaret: See James Matheson and Margaret Sutherland

Sutherland, Margaret: See Jeremiah Sutherland and Margaret Sutherland

Sutherland, Nancy: See Robert Clouston and Nancy Sutherland

Hudson Bay Company Marriages 1820-1851

Sutherland, Robert and Ann Ashim: No. 146, Robert Sutherland, of The Red River Settlement, and Ann Ashim, of The same place, were married at the Grand Rapids, by Banns, with consent of parties, this six Day of February in the year One thousand eight hundred and Forty Six, By me, Wm. Cochran Chaplain to the H. H. B. Company. This marriage was solemnized between us: Robert Sutherland (by mark X), Ann Ashim (by mark X), In the presence of Colin Bruce and John Bruce.

Sutherland, Roderick and Mary Emily Lowman: No. 420, Roderick Sutherland, Bachelor, Red River Settlement, and Mary Emily Lowman, Spinster, of the same place, were married at the White Cottage, by special License, with consent of Parents and Parties, this 18th day of January in the year of our Lord 1849, by me, Wm. Cochran, Chaplain to the H. H. B. Co., Solemnized between us Rodk. Sutherland and Mary Emily Lowman, In the presence of James Lumsden and Mary Ann Cochran.

Sutherland, Sally: See Roderic McKenzie and Sally Sutherland

Sutherland, William and Elizabeth Anderson: No. 189, William Sutherland, of Red River Settlement, and Elizabeth Anderson, of the same place, were married in the Rapid's Church by Banns and with consent of Parties this sixth day of December in the year One Thousand eight Hundred and forty nine, by me, Robert James Missionary. This marriage was Solemnized between us William Sutherland (by mark X) and Elizabeth Anderson, In the presence of William Garrioch and Charles Anderson.

Sutherland, William and Elizabeth Logan: No. 227, William Sutherland and Elizabeth Logan both of the Red River Settlement were married by Banns with Consent of Parties this 31st Day of December 1831, by David T. Jones Chaplain to the Honble. Hudson's Bay Company, Witnesses Present: Robert Logan and James Sutherland.

Sutherland, William and Suzette Trochie: No. 289, William Sutherland, of Red River Settlement, and Suzette Trochie of the same place, were married at Red River by Banns, on the 16th day of December in the year 1834, by Wm. Cockran, 2nd Chaplain to The Honble. Hudson's Bay Compy, Witnesses: Donald Sinclair and Charles Desmarais.

Swain, Betsey: See John McLeod and Betsey Swain

Swain, James and Josette Couteau: No. 287, James Swain, of Red River Settlement, and Josette Couteau, of the same place, were married at Red River Colony, by Banns, on the 7th day of January 1835, By D. T. Jones, Chaplain to the Honble. H. B. Company, Witnesses: Geo. Groat and John Clarke Spence.

Swain, James and Nancy Henry: No. 124, James Swain, of Red River Colony, and Nancy Henry, of the same place, married by Banns at Red River Settlement, on 26 October 1826 by William Cochran, Assistant Chaplain, In the presence of William Garrioch and Peter Corrigal.

Swain, John and Mary Alesie: No. 331, John Swain and Mary Alesie were married at Red River Settlement by Banns with consent of parties on the 18th day of January 1837, by David T. Jones, Chaplain to the Hon. Hudson's Bay Company, Witnesses: Thomas Swain and James Bruce.

Swain, Margaret: See Donald Gunn and Margaret Swain

Hudson Bay Company Marriages 1820-1851

Swain, Margarret: See John Allen Atkins and Margarret Swain

Swain, Mary Anne: See William Robert Smythe and Mary Anne Swaine

Swain, Sarah: See John Macdonald and Sarah Swaine

Swain, Thomas and Eliozabeth Sabiston: No. 382, Thomas Swain, of Red River Settlement and Elizabeth Sabiston of the same place, were married by Banns with mutual consent on the 14th February 1838, by David T. Jones Chaplain to the Honble Hudson's Bay Company, Witnesses: James Swain and Sally Bremner.

Swane, Margaret: See John Favel and Margaret Swane

Tait, James and Mary Lumbere: No. 338, James Tait and Mary Lumbere were married at Red River Settlement by Banns with mutual consent of parties on the 21st day of February 1837, by William Cochran, 2nd Chaplain to the Honble. Hudson's Bay Company, Witnesses: Peter Henderson and Ann Cochran.
Tait, Janet: See Alexander Birston and Janet Tait

Taite, Jane: See John Spence and Jane Taite

Taite, William and Mary Auld: No. 65, William Taite, of York Factory and Mary Auld of the same place were married at York Factory this Tenth day of July on the year, one Thousand Eight Hundred and Twenty Three, by me, John West Chaplain. This marriage was solemnized between us, William Taite and Mary Auld, In the presence of Joseph Spence and John Charles

Tate, Margaret: See John Sutherland and Margaret Tate

Tate, Margaret: See William Bear and Margaret Tate

Tate, Maria: See Henry McCorrister and Maria Tate

Tate, Matilda: See James Irwin and Matilda Tate

Tate, Peter and Jenny Sandison: No. 329, Peter Tate, An Indian, and Jenny Sandison, his reputed wife, were married by Banns with mutual consent on the 9th January 1837, by William Cochran 2nd Chaplain to the Hon. Hudson's Bay Company, Witnesses: Wm. Tate and Fanny Cochran.

Tate, Sarah: See John McKay and Sarah Tate

Tate, William and Mary Bear: William Tate, married 20 Nov 1828, Mary Bear (Cree). (List of HBC Marriages, Joanne J. Hughes, c1977)

Tate, William and Mary: **William Tate and Mary married 13 Feb 1829. (List of HBC Marriages, Joanne J. Hughes, c1977)

Taylor Mary: See John Smith and Mary Taylor

Taylor, Anne: See John Cox and Anne Taylor

Taylor, Anne: See William Harper and Anne Taylor

Taylor, George and Jane Prince: No. 147, George Taylor, Sloope Master, York Factory, married, Julie Prince, a Native of Albany, Hudson's Bay, were married by Banns with mutual consent at Red River Colony on the 11th day of January 1828, by David T. Jones Champlain, Present: Thomas Thomas and William Garrioch.

Taylor, James and Amelia Bird: No. __, James Taylor, bachelor, of Red River Settlement, and Amelia Bird, spinster, of the same place, were married in the Upper Church, by special license and with consent of parties, this twenty thirteenth day of December, in the year of our Lord, one thousand eight hundred and forty Seven, By me, Wm. Cochran. This marriage was Solemnized between us James Taylor and Amelia Bird, In the presence of George Taylor and John Bruce.

Taylor, Jane: See David Harcus and Jane Taylor

Taylor, Jane: See Fredrick Hemmingway and Jane Taylor

Taylor, Margarett: See Aimable Hogue and Margarette Taylor

Taylor, Thomas and Mary Keith: No. 218, Thomas Taylor and Mary Keith, both of Red River Settlement, were married by Banns with Consent of Parties on the 17th of August 1831, by David Jones, Chaplain to the Honble Hudson's Bay Company, Witnesses Present: William Robt. Smith and Wm. Pritchard.

Taylor, William and Sarah Sabiston: No. 131, William Taylor, A Native of the Orkneys and Sarah Sabiston, a Half Breed Woman from the Saskatchewan, were married by Banns with consent of parties at the Protestant Mission Church at Red River Settlement on the 15th day of October 1827 by William Cockan Assistant Chaplain to H.H.B.C., Present: James Slatter, Andrew Setter.

Terresia Bruce: See Peter Spence and Terresia Bruce

Tessot, John Daniel and Salome Knechler: No. 29, John Daniel Tessot, (Swiss) and Salome Knechler (Swiss), were married at York Factory this 28th day of August 1821, by me John West, Chaplain, signed Jean Daniel Tessot and Salome Knechler (x her mark), In the presence of Walton Hausar, Simon McGillivray and Wm. Todd.

Theurer, Anna Regina: See Jacob Witsehy and Anna Regina Theurer

Theya, Mary Margaretta: See Felix Miller and Mary Margaretta Theya

Thomas Thomas and Jane: No. 277, Thomas Thomas, an Indian, now at Red River Colony, and Jane, an Indian woman,, were married by Banns at Red River, on the 8th October 1834, by William Cockran 2nd Chaplain to the Honble. Hudson's Bay Company, Witnesses: Joseph Cook and Jane Johnstone.

Hudson Bay Company Marriages 1820-1851

Thomas, Alexander and Mary Stevenson: No. 397, Alexander Thomas of Red River Settlement and Mary Stevenson of the same place were married at the Indian Settlement by banns with consent of Parents and Parties this eighteenth day of October in the year one thousand eight hundred and thirty eight, by me, Wm. Cochran Asst. Chaplain to the H. H. B. Company. This marriage was solemnized between us Alexander (his X mark) Thomas and Mary (her X mark) Stevenson, In the presence of Joseph Cook and Timothy Bare.

Thomas, Anne: See Alexander Christie and Anne Thomas

Thomas, Anne: See George Bird and Anne Thomas

Thomas, Betsy: See Joseph Bird and Betsy Thomas

Thomas, Catherine: See John Bunn and Catherine Thomas

Thomas, Catherine: See Richard Smith and Catherine Thomas

Thomas, Frances: See Henry Buxton and Frances Thomas

Thomas, Jane: See Levi Bird and Jane Thomas

Thomas, John and Jane Stevenson: No. 398, John Thomas of the Indian Settlement and Jane Stevenson of the same place were married at the Indian Settlement by banns with consent of Parents and Parties this thirty first day of October in the year one thousand eight hundred and thirty eight, by me, Wm. Cochran Asst. Chaplain to the H. H. B. Company. This marriage was solemnized between us John (his X mark) Thomas and Jane (her X mark) Stevens, In the presence of Joseph Cook and Timothy Bare.

Thomas, Richard and Eleanor Thomas: No. 374, Richard Thomas, of Red River Settlement, and Eleanor Thomas, of the same place, were married by Banns with consent of parties, on the 21st day of December in the year 1837, by Wm Cochran 2nd Chaplain to the Hon. Hudson's Bay Company, Witnesses: Jacob Truthwaite and Geo. Steaend [?].

Thomas, Sally: See John Johnston and Sally Thomas

Thomas, Simon and Catherine Linklater: No. 401, Simon Thomas of the Red River Settlement and Catherine of the same place were married at the Grand Rapids RRS by banns with consent of Parents and Parties This sixt day of November, In the year one thousand eight hundred and thirty eight, By me Wm. Cochran Asst. Chaplain to the H. H. B. Company. This marriage was solemnized between us Simon (his X mark) Thomas and Catherine (her X mark) Linklater, In the presence of Ann Cochran and James Taylor.

Thomas, Sophia: See Nicholas Spence and Sophia Thomas

Thomas, Sophia: See Rev. William Mason and Sophia Thomas

Hudson Bay Company Marriages 1820-1851

Thomas, Thomas and Fanny Hope: No. 8, Thomas Thomas and Fanny Hope, both Indians, were married by Banns with consent of parties on the 10th day of December in the year 1835, by William Cockran, 2nd Chaplain to Hudson's Bay Compy., Witnesses: Joseph Cook and Peter Corrigal.

Thomas, Thomas and Harriet Stewart: No. 361, Thomas Thomas Esq, of Red River Settlement, and Harriet Stewart, of the same place, were married at the Upper Church by Banns with Consent of Parents and Parties this Third day of March in the year One thousand eight hundred and Forty One, by me Wm. Cochran Chaplain to the Hon. H. B. Company. This marriage was solemnized between us Thomas Thomas and Harriet Stewart, In the presence of George Gladman and John Bunn.

Thomas, Thomas and Sarah: No. 20, Thomas Thomas, a Principal Settler, of Red River Colony and Sarah of the same place were married at Red River Colony this Thirtieth Day of March in the Year One thousand eight hundred and Twenty-One, By me John West Chaplain, This Marriage was solemnized between us Thomas Thomas and Sarah (x her mark), In the Presence of James Monkman and George Harbidge.

Thomas, Thomas and Sarah: No. 238, Thomas Thomas and Sarah Thomas were married by Banns at Red River Settlement the 25th Day of July 1832, by David T. Jones Chaplain to the Honble. Hudsons Bay Company, Witnesses Present: George Bird and Charles McKay.

Thomas, William and Eleanor Bunn: William Thomas, married 5 Feb 1829, Eleanor Bunn. (Denney)

Thompson, Andrew and Mary Daniel: No. 183, Andrew Thompson, of the Red River Settlement and Mary Daniel, of the same place, were married in the Rapids Church by Banns and with consent of Parties this Fourth Day of July in the year One Thousand eight hundred and forty nine, By me, Robert James Missionary. This marriage was Solemnized between us Andrew Thompson and Mary Daniel (by mark X), In the presence of William Flett (by mark X) and Emma James.

Todd, William and Elisabeth Dennet: No. 418, William Todd Chief Trader in the H. B. Company's service Swan River, and Elisabeth Dennet of the same place, were married at the Grand Rapids, with consent of parties this Twentieth Day of August In the year One Thousand Eight Hundred and Thirty nine, By me William Cochran Asst. Chaplain to the H.H.B. Company. This marriage was Solemnized between us William Todd and Elisabeth Dennet, In the presence of John Slater and John Tait.

Todd, William and Jane Johnstone: No. 188, William Todd, of Red River Settlement, and Jane Johnstone, of the same place, were married in the Rapid's Church by Banns and with consent of Parties this Seventeenth day of September in the year One Thousand eight Hundred and forty nine, by me, Robert James Missionary. This marriage was Solemnized between us Wm. Todd and Jane Johnstone, In the presence of Philip Kennedy and Mary Isbister.

Treathly, Catherine: See Martin Norte and Catherine Treathly

Trochie, Suzette: See William Sutherland and Suzette Trochie

Truthwaite, Elizabeth: See James Richards and Elizabeth Truthwaite

Truthwaite, Isabella: See John Norquay and Isabella Truthwaite.

Truthwaite, Jacob and Elizabeth Vincent: No. 196, Jacob Truthwaite of Red River Settlement and Elizabeth Vincent of the same place, were married at Red River Settlement on the 12th day of March 1830 by Banns with consent of parties, by William Cockran, Chaplain, Present: William Robert Smith and Richard Stevens.

Truthwaite, Jane: See James Anderson and Jane Truthwaite

Truthwaite, Mary: See Thomas Mowat and Mary Truthwaite

Truthwaite, Thomas and Catherine McDermot: No. __, Thomas Truthwaite, bachelor of Red River Settlement, and Catherine McDermot, spinster of the same place, were married at the Upper Church, by banns, with consent of parties, this Eighteenth day of December in the year of our Lord One Thousand, Eight Hundred, and Forty Five, by me John Macdallum, Soliminzed between us, Thomas Truthwaite and Catherine McDermot, In the presence of James Sinclair and John Gunn.

Tunier, Julien and Margaret Grimm: No. 28, Julien Tunier, (Swiss) and Margaret Grimm (Swiss), were married at York Factory this 28th day of August 1821, by me John West, Chaplain, signed Julien Tunier and Margaritte Grimm (x her mark), In the presence of Wm. Williams B Alep. Macdonell B Walton Hausar. Turner, Charlotte: See James Harper and Charlotte Turner

Turner, Francis and Harriette Beardy: No. 11, Francis Turnerr and Harriette Beardy, both of the Indian Settlement, were married by Banns on the 10th day of December 1835, by William Cockran, 2nd Chaplain to Hudson's Bay Compy., Witnesses: Joseph Cook and Peter Corrigal.

Twatt, Elizabeth: See Alexander Bremner and Elizabeth Twatt

Vidnave, Calistique: See Henry Atkinson and Calistique Vidnave

Vincent, Elizabeth: See Alexander Dahal and Elizabeth Vincent

Vincent, Elizabeth: See Jacob Truthwaite and Elizabeth Vincent

Vincent, John and Charlotte: No. __, John Vincent, of the Red River Settlement, and Charlotte of the same place, were married at their Residence, with universal consent on the 21st day of December in the year 1843, by me, Abraham Cowley, Missionary, Solemnized between us John Vincent and Charlotte, Witnesses: Robert Smith and James Sletter.

Vollar, James and Nancy Birston: No. 198, James Vollar, of Red River Colony, and Nancy Birston of the same place, were married by Banns with consent of parties at Red River Settlement on the 18th day of March 1840, by David T. Jones Chaplain and Missionary, In the presence of John Park and James Whiteway.

Wakidge, John and Mary: No. 34, John Wakidge and Mary, of Red River Settlement, were married by mutual consent on the 2nd day of Jun 1836, by David T. Jones, Chaplain to The Hon. H. B. Company, Witnesses: Wm. Tate and William Spense.

Hudson Bay Company Marriages 1820-1851

Walker, Jeannet: See A... Archelle [?] and Jeannet Walker

Walkingchief, Betsy: See John McKnab and Betsy Walkingchief

Walsh, George and Ann Chart: No. 417, George Walsh, Bachelor, pensioner, Red River Settlement, and Ann Chart, Spinster, of the same Place, were married at the Upper Church, by Banns, with consent of Parties this sixteenth day of October, in the year of our Lord, one Thousand Eight Hundred and Forty Eight, by me, W. Cochran, Chaplain to the H. H. B. C., Solemnized between us George Walsh and Ann Chart, In the presence of W. Sharp and C. Stodgell.

Ward, Mary Ann: See Harry Hancock and Mary Ann Ward

Ward, Nancy: See George Spence and Nancy Ward

Ward, Nancy: See John Norquay and Nancy Ward

Warring, John and Lydia Fourniel: No. 36, John Warring of the Red River Colony and Lydia Fourniel of the same place were married at Fort Douglas By Banns, this Eleventh Day of November in the Year One thousand eight hundred and Twenty One, By me, John West, Chaplain, This Marriage was solemnized between us John Warring and Lydia Fourniel, In the Presence of Jno. Alley and A. MacDonald.

Wassaloski, John and Justine Fournier: No. 35, John Wassaloski of the Red River Colony and Justine Fournier of the same place were married at Fort Douglas By Banns, this Eleventh Day of November in the Year One thousand eight hundred and Twenty One, By me, John West, Chaplain, This Marriage was solemnized between us John Wassaloski (x his mark) and Justine Fournier (x her mark, In the Presence of Jno. Alley and A. MacDonald.

White, Joseph and Jane Short: No. 14, Joseph White, of Beaver Creek and Jane Short of the same place were married at Beaver Creek this Twenty-ninth Day of January in the Year One thousand eight hundred and Twenty-One, By me John West Chaplain, This Marriage was solemnized between us Joseph White (x his mark) and Jane Short (x her mark), In the Presence of Alexr Robertson and George McRae.

White, Thomas and Mary Cunningham: No. __, Thomas White, of Fort Pelly, Swan River District, and Mary Cunningham, Red River Settlement were married, at the Upper Church, by special license, with consent of parties, this Third day of July, in the year of our Lord One Thousand Eight-Hundred and Forty Six, by me, John Macallum, Solemnized between us: Thomas White and Mary Cunningham, In the presence of __.

Whitequay, James and Anne Monkman: No. 113, February 20, 1826, John Whitequay, of Red River Settlement, and Anne Monkman, of the same place, were married at Red River Settlement by Banns with consent of parties and parents by David T. Jones Chaplain to The Hon. Hudson's Bay Company In presence of James Monkman and Mr. John Bunn.

Whiteway, James and Chloe Spence: No. 161, James Whiteway, of the Red River Settlement, and Chloe Spence, of the same place, were married in the Rapids Church, by Banns, and with consent of parties, This

Hudson Bay Company Marriages 1820-1851

Third day of February in the year one Thousand eight hundred and Forty Seven by me Robert James Missionary. This marriage was Solemnized between us: James Whiteway and Chloe Spence (by mark X), In the presence of Nicholas Spence and James Park.

Whiteway, Nancy: See James Spence and Nancy Whiteway

Whitford, Anne: See James Sandison and Anne Whitford

Whitford, Charlotte: See John Spence and Charlotte Whitford

Whitford, Eleanor: See Peter Henderson and Eleanor Whitford

Whitford, George and Mary: No. 278, Geo. Whitford, an Indian, now at Red River Colony, and Mary, an Indian woman,, were married by Banns at Red River Settlement, on the 22nd of October 1834, by William Cockran 2nd Chaplain to the Honble. Hudson's Bay Company, Witnesses: Joseph Cook and Catherine Cook.

Whitford, James and Charlotte: No. 269, James Whitford and Charlotte Whitford, were married by Banns at Red River Settlement 5th February 1834, by Wm. Cockran, Assistant Chaplain of the Hon. H. B. Company, Witnesses: Joseph Cook and James Johnston.

Whitford, James and Mary Chlory: No. 103, 29 November 1825, Francis Whitford, of Red River Settlement, and Mary Chlory of the same place, were married at Red River Settlement by Banns with consent of parties by David J. Jones Chaplain to the Hon. H. B. Company, In presence of James Hallet and David Esson.

Whitford, James and Mary Spence: No. 5, James Whitford of the Red River Colony and Mary Spence of the same place were married at Fort Douglas by Banns this Twenty seventh Day of November in the year One thousand eight hundred and Twenty, By me John West Chaplain, This Marriage was solemnized between us Jas. Whitford (x his mark) and Mary Spence (x her mark, In the Presence of Wm. Laidlaw and George Harbidge.

Whitford, Jane: See Samuel Spence and Jane Whitford

Whitford, Mary: See George Sandison and Mary Whitford

Whitford, Mary: See Richard Flett and Mary Whitford

Whitford, Peggy: See George Flett and Peggy Whitford

Whitford, Peter and Christy Spence: No. 6, Peter Whitford of the Red River Colony and Christy Spence of the same place were married at Fort Douglas by Banns this Twenty seventh Day of November in the year One thousand eight hundred and Twenty, By me John West Chaplain, This Marriage was solemnized between us Peter Whitford (x his mark) and Christy Spence (x her mark), In the Presence of Wm. Laidlaw and John Alley.

Hudson Bay Company Marriages 1820-1851

Whitford, Samuel and Mary Henderson: No. 134, Samuel Whitford, of The Red River Settlement, and Mary Henderson, of The same Place, were married at the Grand Rapids, by Banns, with consent of Parents and parties, this Nineteenth Day of December in the year one thousand eight hundred and Forty four By me William Cochran Chaplain to the H. H. B. Company. This marriage was Solemnized between us: John Whitford, Mary Henderson, In the presence of Peter Henderson and John McDonald.

Whitford, Sarah: See William Norn and Sarah Whitford

Whitford, Simon and Maria Spence: No. 201, Simon Whitford, of the Parish of St.Andrews Red River Settlement, and Maria Spence, of the same place, were married in St.Andrews Church by banns and with consent of parties this Twelfth day of December in the year one Thousand Eight hundred and fifty, By me, Robert James Missionary. This marriage was Solemnized between us Simon Whitford (by mark X) and Maria Spence (by mark X), In the presence of Magnus Whitford (by mark X) and John Anderson.

Williams, Joseph and Catherine: No. 340, Joseph Williams and Catherine, his reputed wife were married at Red River Settlement by Banns with consent of parties on the 8th day of March 1837, by William Cochran, 2nd Chaplain to the Honble. Hudson's Bay Company, Witnesses: Joseph Cook and Peter Corrigal. Williams, William and Susannah Williams: No. 23, William Williams and Susannah Williams, of the Indian Settlement, were married by Banns on 24 day of February in the year 1836, by William Cockran, 2nd Chaplain H. B. C., Witnesses: Joseph Cook and Catherine Cook.

Witsehy, Jacob and Anna Regina Theurer: No. 76, May 28th, 1824, Jacob Witsehy, a native of Switzerland and Anna Regina Theurer of the Kingdon of Wirtssemberg, Witnesses: John Allez, Robert Campbell. Marriages celebrated at the Red River Colony from October 1823 to July 1824 by me, David T. Jones 2nd Chaplain.

Work, Alexander and Isabella: No. 78, Alexander Work and Isabella, a Native Indian, were married by Banns at Red River Settlement, on the Thirtieth day of July 1824, By me David T. Jones, Assistant Chaplain, In the presence of: Magnus Birston and William Sinclair.

Work, Betsey: See Henry Budd and Betsey Work

Work, Jane: See John Cunningham and Jane Work

Yorkstone, Charlotte: See John Hodgson and Charlotte Yorkstone

Young, James and Isabella Stevens: No. 174, James Young, of the Red River Settlement, and Isabella Stevens, of the same place, were married in the Rapid's Church by Banns and with consent of parties, This Second Day of November in the year One Thousand Eight huncred and forty Eight, By me, Robert James Missionary. This marriage was Solemnized between us James Young and Isabella Stevens, In the presence of James Gunn and Henry Stevens.

www.ingramcontent.com/pod-product-compliance
Lightning Source LLC
Chambersburg PA
CBHW081228280526
45787CB00006B/2572